Preparing Culturally Informed Educators

Preparing Culturally Informed Educators

Examining Complexities in Practice

Barbara Martin and Susan Foster

ROWMAN & LITTLEFIELD
Lanham • Boulder • New York • London

Rowman & Littlefield
Bloomsbury Publishing Inc, 1385 Broadway, New York, NY 10018, USA
Bloomsbury Publishing Plc, 50 Bedford Square, London, WC1B 3DP, UK
Bloomsbury Publishing Ireland, 29 Earlsfort Terrace, Dublin 2, D02 AY28, Ireland
www.rowman.com

Copyright © 2025 by Susan Foster and Barbara Martin

All rights reserved. No part of this publication may be: i) reproduced or transmitted in any form, electronic or mechanical, including photocopying, recording or by means of any information storage or retrieval system without prior permission in writing from the publishers; or ii) used or reproduced in any way for the training, development or operation of artificial intelligence (AI) technologies, including generative AI technologies. The rights holders expressly reserve this publication from the text and data mining exception as per Article 4(3) of the Digital Single Market Directive (EU) 2019/790.

British Library Cataloguing in Publication Information Available

Library of Congress Cataloging-in-Publication Data Available

ISBN 978-1-4758-7153-1 (cloth : alk. paper)
ISBN 978-1-4758-7154-8 (pbk. : alk. paper)
ISBN 978-1-4758-7155-5 (ebook)

For product safety related questions contact productsafety@bloomsbury.com.

∞™ The paper used in this publication meets the minimum requirements of American National Standard for Information Sciences—Permanence of Paper for Printed Library Materials, ANSI/NISO Z39.48-1992.

Contents

Introduction	1
1 Culturally Informed Instruction—What Is It and What Are the Challenges?	5
2 Culturally Informed Reading Education for All Learners	15
3 Culturally Informed Instruction for Multilingual Learners and All Learners	23
4 Neurological Research and Implications for Cultural Responsivity	41
5 Conclusion: Joining the Movement	47
Appendix A: Writing Development Resources	49
Appendix B: Multicultural Library Development Resources	53
Appendix C: Educational History Surveys	57
References	61
About the Authors	71

Introduction

Today's multicultural and multilingual classrooms reflect an increasingly diverse U.S. population (Compton-Lily et al., 2023; Derman-Sparks et al., 2020; Muhammad, 2023). Indeed, by the year 2060, our country's ethnic and racial minority groups are predicted to constitute the majority of the U.S. population (U.S. Census Bureau, 2023). This demographic juncture calls attention to the need for mainstream educators to be prepared to meet the needs of diverse learners, yet the field of education is inherently limited in this endeavor. Namely, while U.S. classrooms are increasingly heterogeneous, the teaching profession is consistently homogenous. An estimated 79 percent of public school teachers and 72 percent of university professors in educator preparation programs (EPP) are White, and oftentimes mainstream educators have limited exposure to communities outside their own racial, ethnic, linguistic, or socioeconomic backgrounds (Hambacher et al., 2020; Howlett et al., 2017; NCES, 2020, 2024).

Given these circumstances, scholarly research demonstrates the crucial importance of educators' preparedness for increasingly multicultural and multilingual U.S. classrooms (Derman-Sparks et al., 2020; Wei et al., 2022). Concurrently, however, scholarship demonstrates ways in which culturally informed teaching and learning are not well understood or adequately implemented (e.g., see Compton-Lily et al., 2023; Muhammad, 2023; Kane & Savitz, 2022; Ladson-Billings,

2021). Resultantly, a pervasive opportunity gap inhibits many diverse learners' academic achievement and attainment (Faltis & Valdez, 2016; Leider et al., 2021; Lopez & Santibanez, 2018). In the case of Multilingual learners (MLL), our nation's fastest-growing diverse student group, this gap has been characterized as "a persistent and seemingly intractable educational problem" (Leider et al., 2021, p. 3). Also problematic is the mismatch between the norms of home and school that diverse learners oftentimes experience (Smagorinsky, 2013). This mismatch can negatively affect learners' sense of belonging, identity, and academic self-efficacy and, ultimately, can jeopardize their transition into the larger society (Banks, 2020).

These disparities in educational opportunities also deny diverse learners in historically marginalized populations their civil rights guarantee and contradict a federal mandate for equal opportunity, equity, and access (ESSA, 2015a, 2015b; OCR, 1964, 1970). For example, the Every Student Succeeds Act (ESSA) mandates that mainstream teachers have sufficient pedagogical expertise to accommodate diverse learners and to diagnose their needs through multiple means of assessment (ESSA, 2015b, p. 1936). Similarly, Title VI (OCR, 1964, 1970) stipulates that MLLs should not be separated from their English-proficient peers and that English language proficiency cannot interfere with MLLs' academic participation or create an unwarranted special education placement.

In addition to these federal mandates, diverse learners' needs are beginning to be prioritized at the state level. Currently, many states incorporate basic tenets of culturally responsive teaching within professional teaching standards (Muñiz, 2019). However, the majority of states do not articulate a thorough description of culturally responsive teaching practices that is clear or comprehensive enough to support educators' development of instructional practices throughout their careers. To assist educators in this domain, Muñiz (2019) published a list of eight research-based competencies, including:

1. Reflect on one's own cultural lens.
2. Recognize and redress bias in the system.
3. Draw on students' culture to shape curriculum and instruction.
4. Bring real-world issues into the classroom.
5. Model high expectations for all students.

6. Promote respect for students' individual differences.
7. Collaborate with families and the local community.
8. Communicate in linguistically and culturally responsive ways.

Consistent with Muñiz's (2019) guidelines, several states have begun work toward a cohesive integration of culturally informed competencies. In Illinois, for example, Culturally Responsive Teaching and Learning (CRTL) Standards based upon Muñiz's (2019) eight competencies will require EPP to prepare educators who demonstrate self-awareness in their relationships with others (e.g., see *CRTL Standard (a) Self-Awareness and Relationships to Others—Culturally responsive teachers and leaders are reflective and gain a deeper understanding of themselves and how they impact others, leading to more cohesive and productive student development as it relates to academic and social-emotional development for all students*) (Illinois State Board of Education, n.d.).

Illinois educators will also be expected to possess the skills and dispositions to learn about their students' lives outside of school and integrate this knowledge to build instruction that leverages prior knowledge and legitimizes students' backgrounds (Standard a). Additionally, the Illinois CRTL Standards will require EPPs to prepare educators who resist systems of oppression (Standard b), understand students' cultural and linguistic differences to engage with students' families and communities outside of the classroom (Standard c), and forge authentic connections between academic content and students' prior knowledge (Standard d), among others (ISBE, n.d.).

Taken together, these dynamics in education policy and practice underscore the urgent need for EPPs to intentionally prepare culturally informed educators with the knowledge, skills, and dispositions to work effectively with diverse learners. In response to this need, the following chapters represent a vade mecum for EPPs seeking to prepare mainstream educators who can work effectively with diverse learners, families, and communities. Though not intended to represent an exhaustive review of what is required for mastery of culturally informed instruction, this approach does aim to equip mainstream educators with at least the minimum content knowledge, pedagogical skills, and professional dispositions necessary to provide diverse learners with equitable educational opportunities. The following chapters include:

- Chapter 1: "Culturally Informed Instruction: What Is It, and What Are the Challenges?"
- Chapter 2: "Culturally Informed Reading Education for All Learners"
- Chapter 3: "Culturally Informed Instruction for English Learners and All Learners"
- Chapter 4: "Neurological Research and Implications for Cultural Responsivity"
- Chapter 5: "Conclusion: Joining the Movement"

Chapter 1

Culturally Informed Instruction—What Is It and What Are the Challenges?

To prepare mainstream educators who can work effectively with diverse learners, it is important to explore three preliminary questions: (1) What is culturally informed instruction? (2) What are the known challenges associated with understanding and implementing culturally informed instruction? and (3) What does scholarly research say about developing culturally informed educators?

WHAT IS CULTURALLY INFORMED INSTRUCTION?

Culturally informed educators demonstrate the inclination to seek out an understanding of students' cultural, linguistic, academic, and socioeconomic backgrounds (Howlett et al., 2017; Muhammad, 2023). Culturally informed educators must also develop the dispositions to sensitively navigate conflicts that can occur when diverse learners enter school before they have mastered the modes and structures of standard, academic English and the norms of traditional schooling (Faltis & Valdes, 2016). To do so, culturally informed educators must possess the content knowledge and pedagogical skills to craft differentiated instruction that responds to local conditions and accommodates individual student needs, and they must embody the dispositions necessary to sensitively navigate cross-cultural relationships with diverse learners and communities (Gonzales, 2016; Heath, 1982).

Importantly, culturally informed educators also understand that there are complex social and economic dynamics associated with out-of-school influences and unearned social-class disadvantages that can impact diverse learners' academic achievement (Berliner, 2013a, 2013b; Garcia & Weiss, 2015). For example, diverse learners are often from marginalized communities that are historically underserved by the education system (Compton-Lily et al., 2023). As a result, diverse learners are more likely to attend underfunded schools with uncertified teachers and comparatively restricted resources (Shannon, 2014; Wei et al., 2022). Resultantly, in the absence of cultural responsivity, diverse learners who are most in need of differentiated instruction are the very students most likely to receive standardized curriculum that is not culturally responsive (Reinking et al., 2023).

WHY IS CULTURALLY INFORMED INSTRUCTION DIFFICULT TO IMPLEMENT?

In addition to this clear conceptualization, educators who seek to develop cultural responsivity should be aware of the difficulties associated with implementing culturally informed, anti-bias teaching methods (e.g., see Hambacher et al., 2020; Howlett et al., 2017; Kendi, 2023; Walker, 2020). Education scholars have shown that culturally responsive teaching and learning (CRTL) are not well understood or adequately implemented (Kane & Savitz, 2022; Ladson-Billings, 2021b). Culturally informed practices are prone to oversimplification, and they are not easily translated to the large-scale, prepackaged curriculum and standardized assessments that schools serving diverse populations commonly rely on to measure and communicate academic achievement (Paulick et al., 2023). To work effectively with diverse learners, educators need to understand the historical, sociological, and pedagogical complexities associated with culturally informed instruction.

Simplistic Conceptions of Culture

Education scholars find many teachers perceive culture simplistically. For example, they believe ethnic holiday celebrations constitute multicultural education (Sleeter, 2012). Through this simplistic lens, culture is perceived to be embodied in somewhat static and predictable traits such as dances, food, and folklore. In other words, culture is understood only insofar as it can be readily perceived by the senses and in ways that can be fun and exciting to adapt to (e.g., consumer goods) (Hammond, 2015).

These simplistic perceptions tend to highlight between-group differences while neglecting to recognize within-group differences, unspoken cultural norms, and deeply held beliefs that reveal the layered complexities of culture (Pacheco & Gutierrez, 2009). This is problematic because categorizing students based on race, gender, class, or assumptions of cultural traits can reduce individuals to being part of monolithic and, oftentimes, ranked groups (Parks, 2009). Admittedly, simplistic conceptualizations of culture that embrace surface culture can, in some instances, be well intended. However, these perceptions risk reinforcing racialized narratives, stereotypes, and hierarchical thinking. In academic environments, these patterns can interfere with instructional practices by overshadowing variable ways of being that need to be recognized to understand the unique needs and affordances of diverse learners (Brown & Brown, 2012; Ladson-Billings, 2021a).

One-Directional Approaches to School-Community Involvement

Education scholars have also critiqued the one-directional approach to the way schools have traditionally interacted with families and communities. Traditionally, families have been expected to come to school to seek out what they need to know to adapt to the discourses and routines of school (Gonzalez, 2016; Moll et al., 1992). This approach can perpetuate a deficit view of diverse communities by asserting that families from nondominant cultural backgrounds lack worthwhile knowledge and experiences applicable to school (Gutierrez & Rogoff, 2003; Heath, 1982).

This approach is problematic because, as education scholars demonstrate, this one-directional approach has replicated the status quo social hierarchy since schools have not been expected to adapt to the needs of non-elite populations (Avineri et al., 2015; Brion, 2021). In the absence of reciprocity, children who depart from cultural, linguistic, and biological norms are inhibited from achieving a sense of belonging and accomplishment in school and, in some cases, the larger society (Milner, 2021; Smagorinsky, 2013).

Heath's (1983) seminal study of language socialization examined how schools' traditional approach replicated the status quo social hierarchy and failed to adapt to the needs of non-elite populations. For example, in Heath's study of three socioeconomically diverse communities, children in high socioeconomic status (SES) communities were observed being socialized through book-oriented, school-like activities of a formal nature (e.g., reading and discussing a bedtime story) (Heath, 1982). These activities prepared high SES students for a relatively seamless transition into the routines of traditional school. By contrast, children in communities of lower SES tended to be socialized through less formal, more orally based activities that did not provide as seamless a transition into the routines of traditional school. However, Heath (1983) identified myriad ways in which families and communities of lower SES provided multiple means of expression and participation that, if utilized by culturally informed educators, could be equally useful in academic contexts.

Dominant Discourses

In the same vein of thought, education scholars argue that dominant discourses associated with traditional schooling have perpetuated ideological beliefs that consolidate power and privilege for White, European American, upper middle-class learners. These patterns of belief have been found to contribute to discourses of achievement regarding non-mainstream learners that foster low expectations and identity perceptions incongruent with academic achievement (Gee, 2014; Carabello, 2014). Folk Belief Theory, for example, purports that low-advantage students are perceived to be unable to master a rigorous curriculum (Torff, 2014).

These patterns of belief and discourse are problematic because they can have the effect of suppressing educational outcomes in low-advantage schools by reducing the quality and scope of educational resources and opportunities (Torff & Murphy, 2020). By contrast, cultural difference theory challenges the tradition of viewing disparities in social status and educational achievement exclusively through White, middle-class norms. Cultural difference theory calls for an end to stigmatizing those who do not align with such norms as deviant, abnormal, or inadequate (Brown, 2014; Ogbu, 1995).

Pressures of Standardization

Education scholars have also impugned standardization for diminishing multicultural education (Gay, 2013, 2018). Psychometric researchers concur that standardized assessments reduce the scope and quality of content, diminish teacher influence, and distance students from active learning (Shepard, 2016). Of crucial importance to this discussion, these characteristics of standardized assessment practices have been found to unfairly impact students from nondominant cultural backgrounds (Sleeter, 2012; Loveless, 2018).

Moreover, by test makers' own admission, improved standardized test results do not necessarily demonstrate improved achievement or quality of education (Moss et al., 2005; Kohn, 2015). Using NAEP as an example, psychometric researchers explain that standardized assessments are not designed for causal analysis because results do not account for socioeconomic and other factors influencing performance (Moss et al., 2005). Rather, analysis of NAEP scores should be limited to the identification of the jurisdictions within which score divergence is prevalent and where it is not occurring (Carnevale et al., 2019; Wilburn et al., n.d.).

Lack of Research

Finally, there is a lack of research explicitly connecting culturally responsive pedagogy to improved achievement (Kelly et al., 2023; Wei et al., 2022). However, scholars contend that research is not necessary to demonstrate that cultural responsivity is effective pedagogy because there are no monocultural groups of people (Hammond, 2015). Even within seemingly homogenous groups of people, there exists enormous variability in social class, language, sexual preference, and physical ability, among myriad social and individual differences (Gay, 2018; Nieto, 1992).

Hence, academic achievement is necessarily contextual, interactive, personal, cultural, political, and societal (Nieto, 1992). Furthermore, given increasing global interdependence, culturally informed educators are essential to help diverse learners understand their place in society and prevent a mismatch between the cultures of home and school that can interrupt the socialization process and transition into the larger society (Muhammad, 2023).

WHAT DOES SCHOLARLY RESEARCH SAY ABOUT CULTURALLY INFORMED INSTRUCTION?

The challenges associated with culturally informed instruction underscore the deeply complex and historically rooted nature of academic achievement (Avineri et al., 2015). To work effectively with diverse learners, educators must understand these contexts and complexities (Derman-Sparks et al., 2020). To this end, EPP coursework and clinical experiences should be grounded in scholarly research on cultural responsivity for several important reasons.

First, theoretical grounding in culturally informed instruction can bridge learning from college classrooms that are oftentimes culturally homogenous environments to real-world settings with diverse learners (Howlett et al., 2017). The credibility provided by a solid theoretical grounding also substantiates the inherent limitations of largely White college professors from historical and institutional privilege (Derman-Sparks et al., 2020). In the same vein, foundational expertise can preempt potential disinterest and resistance within developing educators who might have limited exposure to communities outside their own racial, ethnic, linguistic, or socioeconomic backgrounds (Hambacher et al., 2020).

A scholarly foundation in cultural responsivity also addresses current policy implications in the field of education. Namely, a theoretical grounding in cultural responsivity demonstrates curriculum alignment with state-mandated *CRTL Standards (e.g., Standard (a) Self-Awareness and Relationships to Others—Culturally responsive teachers and leaders are reflective and gain a deeper understanding of themselves and how they impact others, leading to more cohesive and productive student development as it relates to academic and social-emotional development for all students)* (Illinois State Board of Education, n.d.). The theoretical grounding presented here includes: sociocultural theory (SCT), the interactionist perspective on language acquisition, opportunity to learn (OTL) theory, and the cultural-historical approach.

Sociocultural Theory

SCT is based on Vygotsky's constructivist learning theory and emphasizes the social, cultural, and historical contexts in which learning takes place. According to SCT, just as one cannot live aculturally, one cannot learn aculturally (e.g., see Lantolf & Thorne, 2006; Perry, 2012; Smagorinsky, 2001, 2013; Street, 2013). SCT is a particularly important foundation for culturally informed reading education because it challenges the dominance of some language norms over others. Educators' awareness of the problematic impact of dominant language norms is crucially important for children from nonmainstream cultures who sometimes enter school before they have mastered the modes and structures of standard, academic English (Gonzalez, 2016; Kramsch, 2009). For example, the ability to clearly organize and analyze in an essay-test format (thesis-antithesis-synthesis) has traditionally been awarded educational value (Gee, 2014). By contrast, the context-embedded and associative forms of language and literacy that children from nonmainstream cultures sometimes bring to school, although equally useful in other domains, have at times been devalued in academic contexts (Heath, 1982). Understanding this distinction is uniquely important for delivering culturally informed reading education because the acquisition of standard language norms, or any new set of discourse practices, involves acquiring new identity markers that likely conflict with one's heritage culture (Gee, 2014; also see chapter 2).

The Interactionist Perspective—Accommodating Multilingual Learners

The interactionist perspective on language acquisition offers a timely example of SCT in meeting the instructional needs of MLLs, our nation's fastest-growing diverse student group. The interactionist perspective conceptualizes first and second oral and written language development as a gradual, constructive process that is natural because it is essential for communicating and making sense of the world (Halliday, 1994; Peregoy & Boyle, 2017). This focus is important to preparing educators for the needs of MLLs because it emphasizes the social context of the culture, community, and society in which learners' home languages are nourished and how this process influences the acquisition of a new language (Afflerbach, 2022; Perry, 2012).

Translanguaging. According to the interactionist perspective, learners develop a new language through the process of *translanguaging*. Through *translanguaging*, new language learners use what they know about their home language to develop the new language (Cole, 2019). Research has demonstrated that new language learners analyze similarities and differences in sounds, spellings, print concepts, syntax, and cognates as a way of using their home language to learn a new language (Garcia, Johnson & Seltzer, 2017). In other words, language learners do not develop two languages separately; they necessarily rely on their existing cognitive and linguistic resources to develop bilingually (Gehsmann & Templeton, 2022).

Awareness that new language learners do not develop into two monolingual individuals is crucial to preparing culturally competent educators who understand acquiring English should be additive, not subtractive, of MLLs' first language and cultural identity (Collier & Thomas, 2017; Lopez & Santibanez, 2018). Additionally, while this bilingual approach has been found to benefit MLLs' academic achievement across disciplines, it also improves reading comprehension and cultural competency for English-proficient students (Afflerbach, 2022; August, 2018).

Opportunity to Learn Theory

While SCT and the interactionist perspective are important scholarly groundings for culturally informed pedagogy, cultural responsivity also requires educators' awareness of the environmental context for learning. OTL theory provides this grounding for the environmental domain. It posits that an equitable learning and assessment environment must afford learners similar capacities of action (Gee, 2008).

The study of learning, therefore, necessarily involves the study of learners and their environments. In other words, the learner cannot be considered separately from the environment nor should the learner and the environment be considered distinct factors which can be simply added together to explain development and behavior (Van Der Veer, 2007). Rather, OTL theory contends that knowledge and learning incorporate mind, body, and environment in the way individuals think, feel, act, and interact. Thus, culturally informed educators consider the individual learners and their environments as factors that mutually shape each other in a "spiral process of growth" (Bacon & Kaya, 2018, p. 22).

According to OTL theory, a culturally informed learning and assessment environment must afford all learners similar capacities for action. In other words,

A learner for whom certain objects, people, or features of the environment are not affordances, either because the learner cannot perceive their possibilities for action or cannot affect that action, is not being exposed to the same environment as is a learner for whom these objects, people, or features are true affordances open to the learner's developed or developing affectivity. (Gee, 2008, p. 82)

OTL theory is, particularly, timely given our increasingly multicultural and multilingual U.S. classrooms. Diverse learners' social, cultural, and linguistic backgrounds strongly influence what objects, people, and features of an environment are affordances for learning (Van Der Veer, 2007). In practice, OTL theory addresses our rapidly changing demographics by requiring examination of the ways in which background differences (e.g., socioeconomic, cultural, linguistic) influence what are affordances (e.g., objects, people, features) of a learning environment. Thus, educators demonstrate cultural responsivity by avoiding the assumption that learners have experienced the same OTL through exposure to the same information in the same setting. Rather, culturally responsive educators proactively address potential inequities by seeking awareness of variability in the individual circumstances of diverse learners and adapting to differences in the way objects, people, and environmental features afford opportunities to learn (Hammond, 2015).

The Cultural-Historical Approach

Finally, the cultural-historical approach to the study of cultural variation in learning expands the theoretical framework from the pedagogical (SCT) and environmental (OTL) domains into the societal domain. This theoretical aspect is crucially important because it prepares educators to sensitively navigate cross-cultural relationships with students, families, and communities (Pacheco & Gutierrez, 2009). Specifically, the cultural-historical approach resists conflating ethnicity with culture, and it discourages assumptions that learners carry traits based on their membership in cultural groups (Gutierrez & Rogoff, 2003).

Resistance to these assumptions interrupts reductive notions that are commonplace in educational discourse, such as the idea that group members necessarily carry cultural traits within themselves or that students have predictable learning styles associated with their cultural groups (Gutierrez & Rogoff, 2003; Pacheco & Gutierrez, 2009). This understanding of cultural variation acknowledges that while we naturally expect regularities in cultural communities, we must also expect variation in the way individual group members participate in activities and lived experiences within the group (Dewey, 1938). Educators are challenged to demonstrate cultural responsivity by learning about, from, and with their students, particularly when students are from groups with histories and communities less familiar to them (Freire, 1990).

Specifically, through this approach, educators develop the dispositions to sensitively navigate relationships with diverse learners by becoming mini anthropologists, exploring the lived contexts of students, families, and communities (Moll et al., 1992). In the context of reading education, this approach requires that educators seek an understanding of students' literacy practices across all the contexts of everyday life. For example, educators explore the familial, religious, social, cultural, and political activities learners engage in that involve language and literacy practices, and they identify ways these real-life practices can be utilized as assets and affordances in classroom contexts (Heath, 1983; Pacheco & Gutierrez, 2009).

In this way, the cultural-historical approach aims to replace one-directional relationships reminiscent of traditional schooling with reciprocal relationships in which families have opportunities to learn from schools and schools have opportunities to learn from families (Gonzalez, 2016). Additionally, the cultural-historical approach involves timely implications for education policy. By integrating the cultural-historical approach, EPPs can demonstrate alignment with CRTL Standards (e.g., see *CRTL Standard (f) Family and Community Collaboration—Culturally responsive teachers and leaders will partner with families and communities to build rapport, form collaborative and mutual relationships, and engage in effective cross-cultural communication*) (Illinois State Board of Education, n.d.).

Chapter 2

Culturally Informed Reading Education for All Learners

Literacy development is necessary for acquiring knowledge, for engaging culturally, and for social mobility, and it is arguably the foundation of democracy (Castles et al., 2018). The inability to develop satisfactory literacy skills results in costly personal and economic consequences. For example, low literacy levels have been shown to contribute to inequality through poor physical and mental health, increased likelihood of involvement in crime, and welfare dependency (World Literacy Foundation, 2015). The gravity of consequences associated with low literacy levels involves equity dimensions of reading education and presents important implications for culturally informed instructional practices (Benavot, 2015; Kelly et al., 2021).

Namely, reading instruction that does not adapt to the needs of diverse learners is particularly problematic. A disproportionate percentage of students who strive to read proficiently are culturally, linguistically, and socioeconomically diverse (Compton-Lilly et al., 2023). Additionally, due to rapidly changing U.S. demographics and widening economic disparities, increasing percentages of learners are affected by income and wealth inequality, a primary influencer of academic achievement (Berliner, 2013; Kelly et al., 2021). Students who strive to read proficiently also tend to be from marginalized communities that are historically underserved, often attending underfunded schools with uncertified teachers (Paulick et al., 2023; Shannon, 2014).

Thus, in the absence of culturally informed instruction, striving readers from culturally and socioeconomically diverse backgrounds who are most in need of differentiated instruction are the very students most likely to receive a standardized curriculum that is not culturally responsive (Kane & Savitz, 2022). For these students, it is critically important that mainstream educators are prepared to implement reading instruction that is culturally responsive (Aukerman & Schuldt, 2021; Milner, 2021).

COMPREHENSIVE LITERACY INSTRUCTION.

To deliver culturally informed reading instruction, educators should be prepared for *comprehensive literacy instruction*. The comprehensive approach represents culturally responsive instruction because it prepares educators to teach individual *readers* rather than generically teaching *reading* (Afflerbach, 2022). The comprehensive approach is distinct from other approaches because it is grounded in SCT and is designed to integrate the five pillars of effective literacy instruction (i.e., phonemic awareness, phonics, fluency, vocabulary, and comprehension) (National Reading Panel, 2000).

Comprehensive literacy instruction reflects SCT through awareness of the ways in which literacy is a social practice involving culture and identity (Perry, 2012). *Comprehensive literacy instruction* is constructivist, individualized, adaptable to diverse learners and learning environments, and locally controlled through teachers' expertise and family involvement (Afflerbach, 2022; ESSA, 2015b). This culturally responsive design is reflected in the requirement of quality instructional resources, attention to student interest and background knowledge, differentiated methods, formative assessment, student progress monitoring, and teacher training and planning time (ESSA, 2015b, 2018).

Importantly, the comprehensive approach also prioritizes awareness of family literacy practices (ESSA, 2015b, 2018). As conceptualized in federal literacy policy, *comprehensive literacy instruction* recognizes families as important stakeholders in children's literacy development. To demonstrate this commitment, federal education policy allocates funding to coordinate family involvement with school personnel and to encourage family literacy experiences that support literacy development (ESSA, 2015b, pp. 1941–1942; see also ESSA, 2015a, 2018).

Routman (2000, 2018) describes comprehensive literacy as an instructional model integrating all aspects of language arts while making learning personal, relevant, and authentic. Consistent with SCT, this approach is highly constructivist in the sense that students make meaning through interpreting new experiences rather than learning from others' experiences (Routman, 2000, 2018). In this approach, reading and writing receive daily, sustained emphasis and guided contexts are used to help learners become critical thinkers, independent problem solvers, self-monitors, self-evaluators, and goal setters (Routman, 2000, 2018). Learners are provided choices within clearly defined structures. Skills and strategies are incorporated into real-world learning experiences, and students are provided productive feedback through formative assessment designed to move learners forward. The knowledgeable teacher is part of a professional literacy community culture and serves as a decision maker who, based on students' needs, interests, and experiences, determines when, how, and how much to intervene (Morrow & Gambrell, 2011).

Of crucial importance for diverse learners, *comprehensive literacy instruction* also demonstrates a sociocultural orientation through its shift away from a singular focus on standardized assessments. Multiple means of assessment integrating Universal Design for Learning (UDL) are required to diagnose the needs of diverse learners and Multilingual learners (MLL), monitor students' progress, and inform instruction (ESSA, 2015b, p. 1936). This approach accommodates the assessment needs of students whose literacy skills are below grade level by requiring intensive, supplemental, accelerated, and explicit support (ESSA, 2015b, p. 1942). This requirement prioritizes instruction and assessment rooted in prior knowledge, substantive feedback on ways to improve, and instructional extensions for teaching transfer (Shepard, 2016).

As these descriptions demonstrate, the comprehensive approach aims to integrate many challenging aspects of literacy instruction: reading and writing (rather than focusing heavily on reading at the expense of writing); teacher-directed and student-centered activities (rather than total student inquiry or total teacher-directed instruction); whole-group, small-group, and independent configurations; and skills-focused (e.g., structured phonics instruction) and meaning-focused (e.g., comprehension) instruction. This approach is necessarily adaptable to the learning environment and the unique needs of individual students and ultimately relies on teachers with expertise in literacy instruction and assessment (Morrow & Gambrell, 2011). In practice, the comprehensive approach requires skill in planning, execution, assessment, and reflection by knowledgeable teachers every single day. However, each element is essential for culturally responsive reading instruction, and none should be canceled out (Gabriel, 2018).

Methods and resources to support implementation of the comprehensive approach to reading education include:

- Teach *readers*, not *reading* (Afflerbach, 2022). In all aspects of planning, instruction, and assessment, recognize that comprehension is the ultimate goal of literacy development, and different learners require different pathways to reading proficiency (Elleman & Oslund, 2019; Woulfin & Gabriel, 2022).
- Acknowledge reciprocity among reading processes (e.g., phonemic awareness, phonics and spelling, oral reading fluency, and vocabulary knowledge) (Aukerman & Schuldt, 2021; Morrow & Gambrel, 2011). This can be achieved, in part, through implementing explicit literacy instructional strategies in each of these areas (e.g., see vocabulary instruction strategies for MLLs in chapter 3 and https://textproject.org/teachers/vocabulary-instruction/).
- Similarly, acknowledge reciprocity between reading and writing development (Gehsmann & Templeton, 2022). This can be achieved, in part, through analysis of the six traits of effective writing and through implementing the writers' workshop model. See appendix A.
- Incorporate evidence-based best practices to accommodate the needs of all students in whole-group, small-group, and individualized instruction (e.g., readers' theater, book clubs, literacy circles, and independent reading) (Gehsmann & Templeton, 2022).
- Build on the knowledge, interests, and experiences that students bring to school (Derman-Sparks et al., 2020; Guthrie, Taboada & Wigfield, 2010). This can be achieved, in part, through developing a multicultural classroom library and conducting inventories of readers' interests and motivations (Gehsmann & Templeton, 2022). See appendix B.
- Seek an understanding of students' communities and cultural backgrounds and create opportunities for students to apply literacy strategies for real-world purposes connected to family literacy practices (Paulick et al., 2023). This can be achieved, in part, through

conducting educational history surveys that tap into students' funds of knowledge (Moll et al., 1992). See appendix C.
- Provide authentic assessments in accordance with the diverse strengths and needs of striving readers and MLLs. This can be achieved through qualitative spelling inventories and reading records of word identification, fluency, and comprehension, in addition to methods and materials that accommodate the needs of new language learners (see chapter 3 and Gehsmann & Templeton, 2022).

Finally, a comprehensive approach to reading education demonstrates cultural responsivity through alignment with the federal equity agenda mandated for U.S. public schools. To acquire federal funds for school improvement plans, the Every Student Succeeds Act (ESSA) mandates the implementation of *comprehensive literacy instruction* (ESSA, 2015a, 2015b) (see figure 2.1).

Awareness of this policy and practice alignment is critically important for educators who serve diverse learners and striving readers because the field of reading has experienced a decades-long pendulum swing between conflicting orientations to instructions (Alexander & Fox, 2019). As such, teaching reading is an inherently political endeavor, and reading teachers necessarily navigate the counterproductive terrain of this enduring conflict (Woulfin & Gabriel, 2022). Moreover, the climate resulting from this controversy has precluded innovation and collaboration in the field of reading, which has had damaging implications for diverse learners in need of culturally responsive instruction (Elleman & Oslund, 2019; Torgerson et al., 2019).

Specifically, the pendulum in this debate swings back and forth between a skills-based model of reading instruction and one focused on meaning-making. The skills-based model prioritizes the word recognition aspects of reading development, including phonological awareness and decoding ability (Aukerman & Schuldt, 2021; Shanahan, 2020). While crucially important for literacy development, the word recognition aspects of reading development involve relatively limited attention to individual student needs, experiences, or cultural diversity (Afflerbach, 2022; Compton-Lilly et al., 2023) (see figure 2.2).

Conversely, language comprehension aspects of reading development that are prioritized in the meaning-making model (e.g.,

SEC. 2221. PURPOSES;
DEFINITIONS AND SUBPARTS

Sec.2221.1

"(1) to improve student academic achievement in reading and writing by providing Federal support to States to develop, revise, or update comprehensive literacy instruction plans that, when implemented, ensure high-quality instruction and effective strategies in reading and writing from early education through grade 12;

Sec.2221.2

) for States to provide targeted subgrants to early childhood education programs and local educational agencies and their public and private partners to implement evidence-based programs that ensure high-quality comprehensive literacy instruction for students most in need.

Sec.2221.2a

2a) including developmentally appropriate, contextually explicit, and systematic instruction, and frequent practice, in reading and writing across content areas

Sec2221.2b

2b) includes age-appropriate, explicit, systematic and intentional instruction in phonological awareness, phonic decoding, vocabulary, language structure, reading fluency, and reading comprehension

Sec2221.2c

2c) includes age-appropriate, explicit instruction in writing, including opportunities for children to write with clear purposes, with critical reasoning appropriate to the topic and purpose, and with specific instruction and feed-back from instructional staff

Sec2221.2d

2d) makes available and uses diverse, high-quality print materials that reflect the reading and development levels, and interests, of children

Sec2221.2e

2e) uses differentiated instructional approaches, including individual and small group instruction and discussion

Sec2221.2f

2f) provides opportunities for children to use language with peers and adults in order to develop language skills, including developing vocabulary

Sec2g221.2g

2g) includes frequent practice of reading and writing strategies;

Sec2221.2h

2h) uses age-appropriate, valid, and reliable screening assessments, diagnostic assessments, formative assessment processes, and summative assessments to identify a child's learning needs, to inform instruction, and to monitor the child's progress and the effects of instruction

Sec2221.2i

2i) uses strategies to enhance children's motivation to read and write and children's engagement in self-directed learning;

Sec2221.2j

2j) incorporates the principles of universal design for learning;

Sec2221.2f

2k) depends on teachers' collaboration in planning, instruction, and assessing a child's progress and on continuous professional learning

Sec2221.2l

2l) links literacy instruction to the challenging State academic standards, including the ability to navigate, understand, and write about, complex print and digital subject matter

Figure 2.1 Comprehensive Literacy Policy, ESSA (2015a)

Culturally Informed Reading Education for All Learners   21

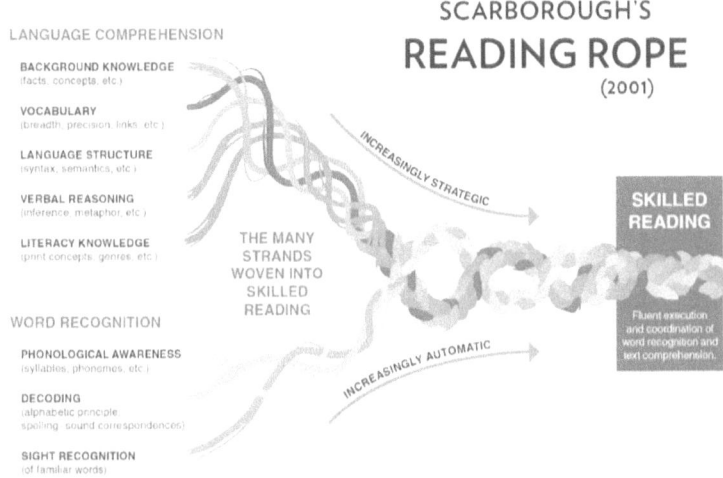

Figure 2.2 Scarborough's Reading Rope (2001)

background knowledge, vocabulary development, language structure, verbal reasoning, and literacy knowledge) are highly attuned to learners' individual needs, interests, and cultural differences (Afflerbach, 2022; Compton-Lilly et al., 2023). *Comprehensive literacy instruction* is historically remarkable because rather than oscillating between the word recognition and language comprehension aspects of reading development, the approach incorporates the continuum of literacy development (e.g., phonemic awareness, phonics, fluency, vocabulary, and comprehension) (Alexander & Fox, 2019; National Reading Panel, 2000). In doing so, the comprehensive approach to reading education accomplishes something essential for diverse learners because it integrates the cognitive, linguistic, social, motivational, and affective factors essential for developmentally oriented, culturally responsive reading education (Aukerman & Schuldt, 2021; Castle et al., 2018; Scarborough, 2001).

Ultimately, the diversity of learners, complexity of the reading process, and importance of prioritizing overall comprehension render it impossible to effectively apply a simple or universal approach to reading instruction that is culturally informed (Kelly et al., 2021; Woulfin & Gabriel, 2022). Rather, the corpus of reading research promotes a robust, socially just approach to reading education consistent with *comprehensive literacy instruction* (Castles et al., 2018; Reinking et al., 2023). This approach is essential to help students from diverse backgrounds learn to decode, comprehend, apply, and critique text while also nurturing literate dispositions such as reading engagement, motivation, and self-efficacy (Aukerman & Schuldt, 2021; Duke & Cartwright, 2021; Elleman & Oslund, 2019).

Chapter 3

Culturally Informed Instruction for Multilingual Learners and All Learners

Of the many diverse learners in need of culturally informed instruction, Multilingual learners (MLL) are the fastest-growing student group (Najarro, 2023). Despite this population trend, mainstream educators are often inadequately prepared to meet MLLs' needs (e.g., see Haas et al., 2016; Kim & Morita-Mullaney, 2020; Kolano et al., 2014; Wei et al., 2022). Indeed, educators report feelings of low self-efficacy and lack of support in meeting MLLs' instructional needs (Najarro, 2023; Polat, 2011).

Additionally, scholarly research has documented that mainstream educators who lack specialized knowledge tend to duplicate standardized curricular goals without accommodating MLLs' language proficiency levels (Kim & Morita-Mullaney, 2020). Research has also documented mainstream educators' tendency to hold deficit views of MLLs, resulting in lower expectations and lessened content rigor (Faltis & Valdes, 2016). Resultantly, MLLs have been found to be misrepresented in special education and underrepresented in academically talented programs (Haas et al., 2016; Wei et al., 2022).

Adding complexity to these troubling conditions is the dearth of educators with specialized EL credentials (Leider et al., 2021). The number of licensed English learner instructors decreased by over 10 percent between 2018 and 2020 (Najarro, 2023). Currently, only around 2 percent of all elementary and secondary teachers are credentialed in English language development (ELD) or bilingual instruction (NCES, 2020, 2024).

Given the pervasive opportunity gap that persists between MLLs and their English-proficient peers, these circumstances highlight an urgent need to prepare mainstream educators with the content knowledge, pedagogical skills, and culturally responsive dispositions necessary to provide MLLs with equitable educational opportunities (Leider et al., 2021). Importantly, preparing mainstream educators to deliver effective instruction for MLLs involves many of the same best practices that improve reading development for native speakers who are striving readers (Afflerbach, 2022; August, 2018). Equally important, culturally informed instruction improves cultural competencies for English-proficient students as well (Banks, 2020; Derman-Sparks et al., 2020).

NURTURING BILINGUALISM

First, to provide MLLs, and all learners, with culturally informed instruction, mainstream educators need preparation in the foundations and methods of first and second language acquisition and learning (Leider et al., 2021). A wealth of scholarly research, including the interactionist perspective on language acquisition, has established that bilingual education programs offer the strongest possibility of closing the EL opportunity gap (Collier & Thomas, 2017; Peregoy & Boyle, 2017). In addition to the benefits of the bilingual approach for new language acquisition, this approach benefits MLLs' academic achievement across disciplines, which is essential for academic success in the upper grades (Morita-Mullaney, 2019).

Importantly, a bilingual learning environment can also improve English-proficient learners' cultural competency by expanding their awareness of diverse cultures and ways of being (Afflerbach, 2022; August, 2018). For example, the following resources enable students to compare words and stories across languages to increase understanding of one another's cultures and lived experiences (Kganesto, 2016):

- The website https://www.lexico.com provides English–Spanish cognate translations within sentences and passages to provide contextual understanding.
- The *International Children's Digital Library* (www.childrenslibrary.org) offers multilingual texts paired with their English counterparts.

NEGOTIATING MEANING

In addition to nurturing bilingualism, culturally informed educators implement strategies that enable new language learners to negotiate meaning in written and oral communication (Gehsmann & Templeton, 2022). This requires establishing comprehensible input for new vocabulary words (Sibold, 2011). Vocabulary knowledge is of particularly critical importance for MLLs' language acquisition and for the content area literacy development that is required for academic success in upper elementary grades and beyond (Peregoy & Boyle, 2017). Likewise, research demonstrates that the same strategies improve reading comprehension and writing composition for English-proficient learners and particularly for striving readers for whom English is their first language (Afflerbach, 2022; Sibold, 2011).

Basic Communication Skills versus Academic Language Proficiency. First, educators must understand important distinctions in vocabulary development. Language learning involves the acquisition of conversational, general academic, and content- or domain-specific academic vocabulary (Peregoy & Boyle, 2017). Conversational vocabulary (also called basic interpersonal communication skills (BICS) or playground language) refers to the language skills needed for interacting with peers in social contexts and negotiating meaning with adults (Beck et al., 2013). New language learners might need explicit instruction in some of these words. However, with minimal instructional intervention, MLLs will often demonstrate baseline competence in conversational vocabulary within six months to two years of arriving to a new country (Gehsmann & Templeton, 2022; Peregoy & Boyle, 2017).

Academic vocabulary involves formal language skills that students will encounter in reading and will need to use in their writing. General academic vocabulary are commonplace words and phrases that occur across content areas. These words and phrases might have high utility in casual conversation but take on different meanings in academic contexts (e.g., product) (Gehsmann & Templeton, 2022; Peregoy & Boyle, 2017).

Conversely, content-specific academic vocabulary words occur infrequently and usually only in specific domains (e.g., species, pollinator, euglossine bees). The relative ease of acquiring BICS can be misleading because, by contrast, learners need substantial time and explicit instruction to develop general and content-specific academic vocabulary knowledge, also known as cognitive academic language proficiency (CALP) (Peregoy & Boyle, 2017). The language skills associated with CALP are crucial for interpreting lectures, formulating arguments orally and in writing, and comprehending academic texts across disciplines at a level commensurate with native speakers (Peregoy & Boyle, 2017). Consequently, to prepare MLLs for reading and writing success in the upper elementary grades and beyond, educators must have the pedagogical knowledge to make academic vocabulary words comprehensible, and they must implement strategies that support literacy development across content areas (Afflerbach, 2022; Shanahan, 2020).

Generating Comprehensible Input.
Comprehensible input refers to pictures, gestures, textual cues, and other extralinguistic information that combine verbal and nonverbal communication channels to make challenging words and concepts more discernible (Peregoy & Boyle, 2017). *Comprehensible input* is essential for MLLs' development of content- and domain-specific academic vocabulary knowledge (Gehsmann & Templeton, 2022).

For example, many MLLs will readily understand the word *happy*, which can provide comprehensible input for understanding the word *content*. Similarly, the word *table* is a common conversational word many new language learners will comprehend. However, in a math or science context, the word *table* takes on academic meaning (e.g., multiplication tables or a way of presenting information or data using rows or columns). For MLLs, understanding the distinction between the word *table* in these differing contexts requires comprehensible input. This input could be generated in the form of a picture of a dinner table, or referring to a table in a classroom, compared to a multiplication table in a mathematic textbook.

In another example, when using the word *airport*, comprehensible input can be created by grouping conceptually related pictures and words such as *tickets*, *baggage*, *cargo*, *loaded*, *runway*, and *pilot* to create a richer learning experience (Gehsmann & Templeton, 2022). Comprehensible input can also be generated by pre-teaching challenging vocabulary words in MLLs' first language, and through bilingual vocabulary journals in which MLLs can rely on cognates and repeated exposures to picture cues (see textbox 3.1) (Sibold, 2011). The website https://wordassociations.net/en is an excellent resource for highlighting semantically and conceptually related word groups with pictures to make vocabulary learning more fertile.

Comprehensible input can also be generated by teaching academic vocabulary kinesthetically, for example, by acting out a word or examining an artifact associated with a word. Similarly, gestures help MLLs comprehend academic language. For example, when using the word furthermore, educators can make a rolling motion with their hands. When demonstrating a comparison or contrast, educators can move one hand with palm facing up and then move the same hand in the opposite direction with palm facing down. When indicating a concluding statement, educators can spread both fingers on both hands and then clasp the hands together (Gehsmann & Templeton, 2022).

Additional methods for generating comprehensible input include establishing background knowledge for challenging words and related concepts through mini lessons. Likewise, small-group oral discussions using new words are essential for allowing MLLs opportunities to practice speaking and listening (Beck et al., 2013; Sibold, 2011). Finally, when MLLs are required to read and write independently, interactive read alouds should be provided to support their ability to access text, and graphic organizers should be used to highlight elements of narrative and informational text (Santora et al., 2016; Witte, 2016). Useful resources that can be accessed by both teachers and learners to provide comprehensible input in the form of visuals, synonyms, pronunciation, and grammatical support include:

- http://www.lexipedia.com/
- http://www.wordhippo.com/
- http://www.youglish.com/

Lowering the Affective Filter.
Comprehensible input is essential for MLLs' academic vocabulary development. However, for strategies to be effective, educators must first reduce learners' *affective filter* so that the input can be received. The *affective filter* refers to the social and emotional influences that affect all learners but which are particularly influential in the acquisition of a new language (Krashen, 1982). Educators can manage these factors through management tools and best practices aimed at creating low-anxiety

environments in which learners feel interested in the content and confident in their ability to progress (Krashen, 1982).

For example, to determine learners' personal interests, motivations, and readiness levels, MLLs should have opportunities to complete interest inventories in their first language, and educators should proactively seek information on learners' previous educational experiences (see appendixes C and D). Teachers should also create bilingual labels for objects, procedures, and directions in the classroom and throughout the school building to reduce MLLs' stress in navigating daily routines. The affective filter can also be lowered by pairing MLLs with a capable classroom partner who can provide guidance and clarification throughout the day (Derman-Sparks et al., 2020).

Respecting the Silent Period.
It is also vitally important to respect the variable silent period of new language learners. A natural silent period allows new language learners to listen and understand speech in authentic contexts without pressure to produce speech or perform rote language drills (Gehsmann & Templeton, 2022). When MLLs begin to write and speak, any level of communication should be celebrated. Early speech and writing are not expected to be grammatically accurate and do not require systematic evaluation at all times (Peregoy & Boyle, 2017).

Implementing Authentic Assessments.
When formal grades are required, assessments should include methods that are non-standardized and of an authentic nature. While standardized assessments are required for measuring and comparing student growth, they have been found to induce anxiety (Ramirez et al., 2016). Standardized testing also reduces the scope and quality of content, reduces teacher influence, and distances students from active learning, all of which have been found to unfairly impact diverse learners (Moss et al., 2005; Rothstein, 2011; Sleeter, 2012). Standardized measures have value in their ease of administration, but they do not provide adequate information for accommodating the needs of diverse learners (Goodman, 2014; Hruby et al., 2011). Hence, to reduce the affective filter, MLLs should be given opportunities to demonstrate learning and growth through multiple means of expression in low-stakes assessment environments (see appendix A) (Gay, 2018; Shepard, 2016).

Diverse Learners and Math Instruction.
Authentic assessments are particularly germane for MLLs' math instruction. Research has demonstrated that providing MLLs with equitable, accessible math instruction involves many of the same instructional considerations as other content areas. For example, like literacy instruction, culturally responsive approaches to teaching math involve high-quality instructional resources, attention to student interest, visual representations for words and concepts, formative assessment, student progress monitoring, and teacher expertise (Boaler, 2008; Spielhagen, 2015).

However, compared to all other subject areas, math carries a distinction that is uniquely important for MLLs. Namely, math learners tend to carry subject-specific anxiety from previous high-pressure experiences. Subject-specific math anxiety has been attributed to standardized assessments that over-emphasize definitive judgments about students' math abilities combined with limited opportunities to engage with mathematics in deep, relevant ways that emphasize critical thinking, real-world connections, and meaningful problem solving (Ramirez et al., 2016). Subject-specific anxiety can follow students throughout their academic careers and have significant impacts on their attitudes and self-perceptions of math ability (Jackson, 2016; Spielhagen, 2015).

Given what we know about how strongly social-emotional factors affect new language acquisition and, particularly math education, equitable instruction for MLLs requires taking action to create a low-anxiety learning and assessment environment (Aguirre et al., 2013; Martin et al., 2010). Importantly, however, subject-specific anxiety and overall stress can affect all learners. As a result, culturally informed instruction and assessment that reduces stress and lowers the affective filter is beneficial for all learners (Krashen, 1982).

DISPOSITION AND INCLINATION

Examining Cultural Complexity.
In addition to the instruction and assessment accommodations reviewed here, learning a new language necessarily involves acquiring new identity markers that likely conflict with the norms of one's heritage language and culture (Gee, 2014). Thus, mainstream educators need the cultural competency to sensitively navigate conflicts that can occur

when MLLs enter school before they have mastered the modes and structures of academic English and the norms of traditional schooling (Faltis & Valdes, 2016; Gonzalez, 2016).

This requires educators to resist assumptions about the sameness of individuals within cultural groups. Rather, culturally competent educators explore variation in the way individual group members participate in activities and lived experiences within groups (Dewey, 1938). To do so, educators must develop the dispositions and demonstrate the inclination to sensitively navigate cross-cultural relationships with MLLs and their families and communities (Gutierrez & Rogoff, 2003; Pacheco & Gutierrez, 2009).

Hammond's (2015) *Culture Tree* exercise (see figure 3.1) represents an effective strategy by which educators can examine their students' context for learning and intentionally seek deeper understanding of diverse learners' unique backgrounds (Howlett et al., 2017;

Figure 3.1 Culture Tree (Hammond, 2015)

Muhammad, 2023). This exercise nurtures awareness of cultural complexity on three levels: surface culture, unspoken rules, and deeply held beliefs.

- Surface culture refers to elements that are easy to see, smell, and taste.
- Unspoken rules refer to the social norms of culture that which might be considered common sense and which govern the way members of the group interact and build trust.
- Deeply held beliefs refer to core values (e.g., ethics, power, love) of a culture group that members might not consciously grasp but which can strongly influence one's worldview (Hammond, 2015).

In lesson planning, educators can apply this analysis to prepare curriculum and instruction that considers differences in culture, language, and socioeconomic status for MLLs and for all learners (see textbox 3.1). Additionally, this exercise can be implemented within educator preparation classrooms that are often comprised of professors and teacher candidates from homogenous backgrounds. In the college classroom context, future educators can develop cultural competency by discovering the myriad within-group differences that often exist among mostly female, White college students (Hambacher et al., 2020; Nieto, 1992).

EXAMPLE LITERACY LESSON PLAN WITH DIVERSE LEARNER ACCOMMODATIONS

Grade Level: Fourth Grade	
	Summary of lesson: The purpose of this lesson is for students to practice recounting an experience in an organized manner using relevant facts and descriptive details that support a main idea. Students will also practice retelling their experience by speaking clearly at an understandable pace. (CCSS.ELA-LITERACY.SL.4.4)
	Students will also include pictures (visual displays) in their presentations to enhance the development of main ideas and themes. (CCSS.ELA-LITERACY.SL.4.5)
	In this lesson, students are recounting their recent experience of a field trip to a local nature center. Students' presentations follow the structure of a teacher-led mini lesson, guided by a partially complete story organizer.
	In this lesson, the teacher will accommodate the MLL by pre-teaching academic vocabulary words and allowing the MLL time to enter the new words in a bilingual vocabulary journal with picture cues. Also, the MLL is accommodated by working/presenting with a partner and by drawing pictures that create comprehensible input for new ideas. The MLL will also complete the summative assessment in the first language before translating it to English with teacher support.

Part 1: Context for Learning: Describe the learning community of your whole class.	**What do you know about your students, their learning strengths/needs, background knowledge, and interests?** This group of students is very interactive and supportive of each other. They show strong interest and engagement with the curriculum when they work together in small groups and pairs. They are chatty and perform well when they can move around and cheer each other on. They need to develop the ability to work more independently and maintain their focus in a quiet environment. We are working on mindfulness techniques to reflect on our independence and improve focus. We have one Multilingual learner (first language Spanish) who receives sheltered English instruction several times a week and one student who receives accommodations for a language processing difference. We also have one student who receives social-emotional accommodations. We have five students who are consistently early finishers and require extensions. Our early finishers are often strategically paired with our MLL to provide support and clarification throughout the day.
Part 1a: Context for Learning: Describe your Multilingual learner(s)' *Culture Tree* (Hammond, 2015)	**What can you observe about your MLL(s)' surface culture?** Our MLL's first language is Spanish. He likes animals and nature and will often choose reading materials on these topics. He also likes music, and although he is speaking very little English in the classroom, he will sing in English to himself and with his classmates. He is well-liked and very socially engaged with his classmates. **What have you discovered about your MLL(s)' unspoken cultural rules?** Our MLL is Catholic, and he has a large, extended family community who work together in a local family business. Based on my observations so far, our MLL's family prioritizes education. Initial assessments showed our MLL is at grade-level proficiency in Spanish, and he consistently completes homework assignments at a satisfactory level. **What have you discovered about your MLL(s)' deeply held beliefs?** At this time, most of our MLL's extended family communicates only in Spanish. Our MLL has an older sister who has developed English proficiency quickly, and she serves as the representative for the family in all their communications with the school. I believe our MLL's sister helps him with homework assignments. Because our MLL's extended family does not communicate readily with the school, I have not had opportunities to learn more about their deeply held beliefs. However, I am seeking opportunities to communicate with the family more frequently through a translator who volunteers for our school.

Part 2:	What is the full standard(s)?
Common Core State Stanadard—ELA/Literacy Standard (CCSS) https://www.thecorestandards.org/ELA-Literacy/	Presentation of Knowledge and Ideas: CCSS.ELA-LITERACY.SL.4.4 Report on a topic or text, tell a story, or recount an experience in an organized manner, using appropriate facts and relevant, descriptive details to support main ideas or themes; speak clearly at an understandable pace. CCSS.ELA-LITERACY.SL.4.5 Add audio recordings and visual displays to presentations when appropriate to enhance the development of main ideas or themes.
Culturally Responsive Teaching & Learning Standard (CRTL) https://www.isbe.net/Pages/Culturally-Responsive-Teaching-Leading-Standards.aspx	CRTL Standard c. Understand students' cultural and linguistic differences to engage with students' families and communities outside of the classroom. CRTL Standard d. Forge authentic connections between academic content and students' prior knowledge.
	Will you address the full standard or only part for the whole class? The focus for the whole class is on recounting their field trip experience in an organized manner providing relevant, descriptive details to support the main idea, with pictures that enhance the development of the theme. Through pairs' choral reading, the teacher will also evaluate students' speech for a clear and understandable pace.
	Will you address the full standard or only part for your MLL(s)? For our MLL, the focus will be limited to recognizing relevant, descriptive details that support the main idea. If our MLL is not comfortable speaking during the choral read, I will not evaluate for a clear and understandable pace. The choral reading exercise will serve as an opportunity for our MLL to practice listening skills.

Culturally Informed Instruction for Multilingual Learners and All Learners 35

	Describe any specific methods planned for lowering your MLL(s)' affective filter during this lesson:
	Our MLL will have the support of a partner and a partially completed story organizer, and our MLL will not be pressured to read aloud in the choral reading exercise. This will lower the affective filter by respecting our MLL's silent period and allowing practice in listening. The exercise also involves drawing pictures to represent story elements which will create comprehensible input and engagement, helping to lower the affective filter. In the summative assessment, our MLL's affective filter will be lowered by completing the assignment first in their first language, before translating the assignment to English in class with teacher support.
Part 2a: Leveled Objectives: **Create leveled objectives that are clearly aligned with your standard.** **Every student must meet the basic objective.** **Identify which objective is the goal for your MLL(s): Basic**	Use "ABC" Format: The [Actor] will [Behavior of Language Function] by [Conditions Description] a. **Basic**—Students will be able to work with a partner to recount an experience in writing in an organized manner that includes relevant, descriptive details supporting a main idea. b. **Whole Class Goal**—Students will be able to work with a partner to recount an experience in writing in an organized manner that includes relevant, descriptive details supporting a main idea. Students will also be able to create pictures that enhance the theme of their presentations. Students will also be able to orally retell their experience in a clear and understandable pace. For homework, students will be able to work independently to recount an experience in writing in an organized manner that includes 2 relevant descriptive details supporting a main idea. c. **Early Finishers**—objective involving extensions/explorations for students who have demonstrated mastery of basic and whole class goal objectives (include an explanation of extended resources and materials). Early finishers who complete the homework assignment in class will be assigned an extension activity (see summative assessment).

| Part 3: Assessment System: Create a timeline that includes formative assessments you use to gauge interest/needs, set goals, monitor progress, provide feedback, and reflect on necessary adjustments throughout the learning process. | • **Assessment activities before lesson begins (formative)**

In an introductory mini lesson, the teacher retells her own childhood field trip experience (see teacher-led mini lesson, part 6). After the teacher completes the mini lesson, students receive a paper copy of the retell. To pre-assess students' readiness for identifying relevant, descriptive details that support the main idea, students are asked to underline the main idea in red and to underline relevant, descriptive details in green. Students are asked to underline irrelevant details in yellow.

MLL Accommodation: The teacher provides a home language translation (Google Translate) of the mini-lesson story before whole class instruction. MLL students will also be given time to enter content area vocabulary words with picture cues in a bilingual vocabulary journal before whole class instruction begins (see part 4).

Translator: (https://translate.google.com/?sl=auto&tl=en&op=translate)

• **Assessment activities during lesson (formative)**

Student pairs will recount their own field trip experience using a partially completed story organizer to guide the organization of their ideas (see story organizer, part 6). The teacher will formatively assess students' progress by evaluating the choral reading of students' stories and students' responses to the teacher's questions regarding the main idea and relevant, descriptive details.

• **Assessment activities upon lesson completion (summative)**

Students will complete an independent written homework assignment in which they recount a past educational experience. Following the same story structure, students will explain what they learned that made their experience educational (main idea) and provide two relevant/descriptive details to support their main idea. |

	MLL Accommodation: Our MLL students will complete the summative assessment in their first language and then translate the assignment to English during class time with teacher support. **Early Finishers Accommodation:** Early finishers who complete the summative assessment during class time will be assigned the following extension for homework: Explore the questions below using the resources: **https://www.chop.edu/news/health-tip/recognizing-poison-ivy-oak-and-sumac** https://my.clevelandclinic.org/health/diseases/10655-poison-plants-poison-ivy--poison-oak--poison-sumac About what percentage of people are allergic to poison ivy, poison oak, and poison sumac? About how much exposure to these plants will cause a rash? What types of people are commonly exposed to these plants? How should a person treat the rash from these poisonous plants?
Part 4: Bilingual Vocabulary Supports	1. **List tier 2 words:** High frequency, multiple meaning, and general academic words • commonplace words and phrases with high utility in casual conversation, but they can take on special meaning in particular contexts or disciplines (e.g. product) nature/natural—naturaleza/ naturales. relevant/irrelevant—importante/ irrelevante descriptive—descriptivo main idea—la idea principal descriptive details—descriptivos common—común poisonous—venenoso **Useful Cognates:** natural/naturales, importante (relevant), irrelevant/irrelevante, venenoso/venomous

2. **List tier 3 words:** Low frequency, subject-related, domain-specific academic words.
   - technical terms that occur infrequently outside of disciplinary contexts (e.g., species, pollinator, euglossine bees)

   poison ivy—hiedra venenosa
   poison oak—hiedra venenosa
   poison sumac—zumaque venenoso

   Pictures (links) for use in bilingual vocabulary journal:
   https://kids.niehs.nih.gov/topics/natural-world/wildlife/plants/poison-ivy

3. **List materials/methods/resources planned for generating comprehensible input, such as:**
   - anchor charts
   - word walls
   - experiments/field trips—*Nature Center Field Trip*
   - multisensory input (visual aids/gestures/acting out): *Students will draw pictures of the 3 poisonous plants*
   - graphic organizer—*partially complete story organizer*
   - note taking aid
   - partner/strategic grouping—*strategic pairs and choral reading*
   - oral practice—*choral reading of completed story*
   - digital resources: online modules, online read-alouds, recordings/translations: https://youtu.be/Rcg7C1IRq8w

   https://youtu.be/hxs3TNn6EJQ

Part 5: Adaptations in Content, Process & Product	Content—How will you adapt the lesson content *the subject matter being covered*—to meet the needs of your Multilingual learner(s)?
	For our MLL, I will not expect to evaluate oral speech for clear and understandable pace. If needed, I will respect our MLL's silent period and allow our MLL to practice listening during the choral reading exercise. For our MLL, I will focus the content on our MLL's ability to identify relevant, descriptive details that support a main idea.
	Process—How will you adapt the lesson processes *the activities planned*—to meet the needs of your Multilingual learner(s)?
	- I have translated the mini lesson into our MLL's first language. - I have translated the academic vocabulary words into our MLL's first language and provided time for our MLL to enter the vocabulary words with associated picture cues in the bilingual vocabulary journal. - I have provided a story organizer to guide our MLL in the structure of the assignment. - I have provided digital resources for our MLL to review the content of the assignment: https://youtu.be/hxs3TNn6EJQ, https://youtu.be/Rcg7C1Rq8w
	Product—How will you adapt the lesson product—*the culminating expectations of the lesson (assessment, project, portfolio etc.)*—to meet the needs of your Multilingual learner(s)?
	Our MLL will complete the summative assessment in their first language (homework). I will have a one-on-one conference with our MLL to translate the summative assessment into English during class time.

Part 6: Materials	Teacher-Led Mini Lesson

	When I was in the fourth grade, I went on a field trip that I will never forget. My class traveled to Springfield, Illinois, to experience the president Abraham Lincoln historical sites. The field trip was educational, but it was also great fun!
	
	Our bus trip to Springfield, Illinois, was almost three hours long. I had such fun on the bus with my friends. We listened to music, ate snacks, and played games. The bus was yellow.
	
	Of course, I learned many interesting and important facts about President Abraham Lincoln on my field trip. However, most of all I remember the fun we had on the bus. Maybe I will take my own fourth grade class on the same field trip very soon!
	
	Story Organizer—Student Pairs
	
	Hello, our names are _____. We are fourth graders at _____ school. Our class recently went on a field trip to a nature center called _____. This field trip was fun, and it was also educational. The field trip was educational because we learned about 3 types of common plants which are _____. The 3 plants are called _____, _____, and _____. If you touch these plants, you might _____. You can identify these poisonous plants by the shapes and textures of their leaves.
	
	Using the resources below, draw and describe the leaves of each of the plants.
	• https://youtu.be/hxs3TNn6EJQ
	• https://youtu.be/Rcg7C1lRq8w
	• https://kids.niehs.nih.gov/topics/natural-world/wildlife/plants/poison-ivy)
	
	          Poison Ivy Poison Oak
	                  Poison Sumac

Chapter 4

Neurological Research and Implications for Cultural Responsivity

Today's culturally informed educators have the benefit of burgeoning neuroscientific research that is improving our understanding of how brain functioning impacts learning (Degen, 2014; Ludvik, 2023). This understanding has important implications for diverse learners (Hammond, 2015). Namely, instructional practices that are informed by neuroscientific research-support brain-friendly environments that make learning more accessible for all students (e.g., see Derman-Sparks et al., 2020; Hruby et al., 2011; Tomlinson, 2017). Thus, as part of developing cultural responsivity, educators should plan instruction and optimize classroom environments based on the findings of recent neuroscience (Sousa & Tomlinson, 2018).

THE BRAIN AND STRESS

The primary job of the brain is to keep its owner alive. When stimuli are interpreted by the brain to be a threat to survival (anger, fear, anxiety), a reflexive response (adrenaline) shuts down unnecessary activity and directs the brain to the source of the stimuli (Sousa & Tomlinson, 2018). Under stressful conditions such as high-stakes summative testing, the hormone cortisol is elevated, and the brain's frontal lobe stops processing low-priority information not needed for survival. This can have an inhibitory effect on academic learning because cortisol suppresses recall of information from memory (Endres et al., 2017). When stress is lessened, however, cortisol levels reduce and endorphins increase, allowing the frontal lobe to focus on academic learning rather than survival alone (Sousa & Tomlinson, 2018).

The unstressed brain is reflective rather than reflexive. This is a critical distinction because reflection is essential to the most fundamental mechanism of learning. When students learn new information, their brain cells (neurons) activate (fire) and begin connecting (synapse) with other neurons. Hence the expression "neurons that fire together, wire together" (Ludvik, 2023). As students rehearse new concepts, neurological synapses strengthen, and the new information becomes more easily retrievable for connection and application (Ludvik, 2023). Ultimately, a reflective brain builds cognitive networks more efficiently, recalls information more readily, and can ultimately more easily connect new concepts to previous learning and apply new concepts for future learning (Sanchez-Ruiz et al., 2015).

Additionally, learning environments that are sensitive to the neurological impacts of stress are particularly important for students who have experienced adverse childhood experiences (ACE). ACEs can result from the repeated stress of abuse, neglect, or parents struggling with mental health or substance abuse issues, among others (see figure 4.1). These stressors have been found to have tangible, measurable effects on children's cognitive, emotional, and brain development (see https://www.ted.com/talks/nadine_burke_harris_how_childhood _trauma_affects_health_across_a_lifetime?subtitle=en). Examining students' ACEs is critically important because neurological research on brain plasticity has demonstrated that when these stressors are identified and attenuated, educational interventions can be effective (see https:// www.ted.com/talks/kimberly_noble_how_does_income_affect_child- hood_brain_development?subtitle=en). However, absent identification and intervention, ACEs can have long-term, negative effects on health, opportunity, and well-being (Maguire-Jack et al., 2021).

INSTRUCTIONAL CONSIDERATIONS

Identify Learners' ACEs.

ACEs can result from stressors that are common to all populations of learners. However, ACEs are more likely to be experienced by some student groups than others. Specifically, researchers have identified an

Adverse Childhood Experiences (ACEs) Checklist

The most important thing to remember is that the ACE score is meant as a guideline: If you experienced other types of toxic stress over months or years, then those would likely increase your risk of health consequences, depending on the positive childhood experiences you had. Please a check mark by the experiences you had prior to 18 years old:

- ☐ Did a parent or other adult in the household often or very often... Swear at you, insult you, put you down, or humiliate you? or Act in a way that made you afraid that you might be physically hurt?
- ☐ Did a parent or other adult in the household often or very often... Push, grab, slap, or throw something at you? or Ever hit you so hard that you had marks or were injured?
- ☐ Did an adult or person at least 5 years older than you ever... Touch or fondle you or have you touch their body in a sexual way? or Attempt or actually have oral, anal, or vaginal intercourse with you?
- ☐ Did you often or very often feel that ... No one in your family loved you or thought you were important or special? or Your family didn't look out for each other, feel close to each other, or support each other?
- ☐ Did you often or very often feel that ... You didn't have enough to eat, had to wear dirty clothes, and had no one to protect you? or Your parents were too drunk or high to take care of you or take you to the doctor if you needed it?
- ☐ Were your parents ever separated or divorced?
- ☐ Was your mother or stepmother: Often or very often pushed, grabbed, slapped, or had something thrown at her? or Sometimes, often, or very often kicked, bitten, hit with a fist, or hit with something hard? or Ever repeatedly hit over at least a few minutes or threatened with a gun or knife?
- ☐ Did you live with anyone who was a problem drinker or alcoholic, or who used street drugs?
- ☐ Was a household member depressed or mentally ill, or did a household member attempt suicide?
- ☐ Did a household member go to prison?

A high ACE score increases risk of negative long term impacts on health, opportunity and well being. An ACE score of 4 or more, increases potential negative impacts on cognitive, emotional and brain development.

Please note that this is not an exhaustive list of trauma that can be considered an adverse childhood experience.

References
https://www.cdc.gov/aces/about/index.html
https://acestoohigh.com/got-your-ace-score/
Kalmakis, K. A. & Chandler, G. E. (2015). Health consequences of adverse childhood experiences: A systematic review. Journal of the American Association of Nurse Practitioners, 27(8), 457-465.

Figure 4.1 ACEs checklist

association between ACEs and concentrated neighborhood poverty, as well as parenting stress (Maguire-Jack et al., 2021; Steele et al., 2016). Thus, culturally responsive educators should inform themselves about student groups that are most likely to be affected by ACEs and their potential impact on children's cognitive, emotional, and brain development (see https://www.cdc.gov/aces/about/index.html). The following survey can be utilized as one measure of learners' ACE scores (see https://acestoohigh.com/got-your-ace-score/).

Incorporate Student Choice and Authentic Assessment.
Given our understanding of how standardized assessments can unfairly impact diverse learners (e.g., see Moss et al., 2005; Ramirez et al., 2016; Rothstein, 2011; Sleeter, 2012), culturally informed educators should implement authentic assessments that tap into learners' personal interests and prior experiences (Reeves, 2016; Shepard, 2016). Degen (2014) explains that knowledge is developed when students connect to information and answer real-world questions that "are driven by their own purpose, interest, and need to search for meaning" (p. 7). Thus, learners should have opportunities to apply information in meaningful ways and to demonstrate growth through multiple means of expression (Sousa & Tomlinson, 2018).

For example, rather than requiring all students to write a traditional book report, create a list of projects from which students can choose that reflect their interests and optimize their strengths. Could students create a visual map that illustrates key settings in the book and add specific details for what happened at each juncture? Perhaps students would be more interested in converting the story into a play or creating an infomercial marketing the book. Providing variable options can stimulate a brain-friendly environment in which learners' reflective brains apply and connect information rather than reflexive brains that are preoccupied with test scores (Reeves, 2016).

Importantly, these assessments are brain-friendly for all learners because authentic methods encourage intrinsically motivated *learning goals* rather than extrinsically motivated *performance goals*. *Learning goals* are focused on task, not ego. As a result, *learning goals* have been shown to result in skills mastery more often because mistakes are perceived to be a natural part of the learning process (Elliot & Dweck, 2005). By contrast, *performance goals* tend to have high ego involvement due to the extrinsic motivation to outperform others. *Performance goals* have been found to result in skills mastery less often because failure implies a lack of ability (Elliot, 1999). Hence, *learning goals* are brain-friendly because they reward risk-taking and growth, while *performance goals* tend to create a helpless response pattern and a mindset that is not conducive to learning (Sousa & Tomlinson, 2018).

Consider Physiological Rhythms.
Every individual has unique physiological rhythms (Jensen, 2008). Observing learners' natural patterns and planning instruction accordingly

can optimize productivity. Jensen (2008) recommends varying when different subjects are taught so that students who thrive at different times of the day have opportunities to learn during periods of peak performance. For example, as part of designing authentic assessments, vary the times of the day students can choose to complete formative and summative evaluations to increase accuracy in measurement.

Neuroscientific research also finds instruction is best received in twenty-minute increments. Medina (2008) created a ten-minute rule for teachers to consider in planning. Each instructional section lasts only ten minutes and covers an individual core concept. Maintaining this ten-minute instructional routine will increase brain friendliness by encouraging teachers to be concise, and it will deliver information in intervals that accommodate learners' physiological rhythms.

CREATE LEARNER PROFILES

Culturally informed educators should apply neurological research to learner profiles that inform classroom management, planning, and instructional choices (Sousa & Tomlinson, 2018). Learner profiles should integrate the following:

- Evaluation of learners' ACEs.
- Provide families and caregivers with information on ways to attenuate the effects of ACEs.
- Observe differences in how learners approach learning (e.g., analytically or creatively).
- Observe differences in learners' preferences related to subject, topic, time of day or year, and other factors related to natural physiological rhythms (e.g., independence or collaboration, stillness or movement).
- Vary instructional modes and create opportunities that accommodate learning preferences (e.g., direct instruction, small group, linear, expressive).
- Provide opportunities for students to express learning in a variety of modes (e.g., authentic assessment, oral/written expression, digital/multimodal).
- Encourage learners to become self-aware of approaches that do and do not work for them (e.g., part to whole or whole to part, competition or collaboration).

- Take interest surveys, conduct parent/caregiver interviews, and create opportunities to discuss identities and cultural backgrounds as a means of informally assessing prior knowledge.
- Nurture a classroom community that embraces differences as assets (Dack & Tomlinson, 2015; Sousa & Tomlinson, 2018).

Put succinctly, different people approach learning differently (Bondie et al., 2019). Culturally informed educators understand this, and they do not attempt to implement one-size-fits-all instruction or assessment (Banks, 2016; Gay, 2013). Recent neuroscientific research supplements this understanding in ways that can significantly reduce learners' stress and create optimal, brain-friendly learning environments (Sanchez-Ruiz et al., 2015). Moreover, the application of neuroscientific research can counteract common stressors known to impact children's cognitive, emotional, and brain development, increasing learners' academic attainment and improving their overall life trajectories (Maguire-Jack et al., 2021; Steele et al., 2016).

Conclusion
Joining the Movement

Teachers and learners in today's multilingual and multicultural U.S. classrooms are facing more challenges than ever before. These challenges cannot be adequately addressed without educators who are prepared to deliver culturally informed instruction and assessment. However, there is very little uniformity in educator preparation across the United States (Goodson et al., 2019; Villegas & Pompa, 2020). While many states are beginning to prioritize diverse learners' needs through culturally responsive teaching and learning standards, expectations for practicing and licensing educators remain relatively inconsistent within and between states (Muñiz, 2019).

This inconsistency is particularly salient in the case of Multilingual learners (MLL). Despite a dearth of credentialed instructors with the expertise to meet MLLs' needs, only twenty-one state education agencies (SEA) make any reference to MLLs in the language of their professional standards (Leider et al., 2021). In states that require a credential beyond initial licensure for educators to be designated MLL teachers, the standards are of highly variable quality. Additionally, earning a specialized credential in MLL instruction sometimes creates an unequal financial burden for educators who proactively seek this expertise (Leider et al., 2021).

Given these complex dynamics, it is unrealistic to expect educators to singlehandedly remove obstacles to learning. With necessary preparation, however, educators can ensure that their instructional choices thoughtfully consider how to reach students with diverse prior knowledge and who are from a wide variety of backgrounds with unique lived experiences. To achieve this, it is incumbent upon professionals in teacher training to prioritize culturally informed practices. EPPs must methodically infuse mainstream educator preparation with the minimum content knowledge and pedagogical expertise necessary to provide diverse learners equal educational access (Kim & Morita-Mullaney, 2020; Wei et al., 2022).

This manual has offered an inside view of how one Midwestern EPP has thoughtfully considered Muñiz's (2019) culturally responsive teaching competencies, as well as the state-mandated Illinois CRTLs, to achieve this aim (ISBE, n.d.). This view does not represent an exhaustive integration of what comprises expertise in culturally informed instruction. It does, however, explore one small-scope example of how EPPs can equip mainstream educators with the minimum content knowledge, pedagogical skills, and culturally responsive dispositions necessary to provide diverse learners with the equitable educational opportunities and access that they are guaranteed by the U.S. federal government (ESSA, 2015a, 2015b; OCR, 1964, 1970).

At a basic level, this infusion lays the groundwork for how educators can individualize instruction and begin to plan for culturally responsive instruction and assessment. According to Muñiz (2019), "Culturally Responsive Teaching involves connecting academics to students' daily lives, cultural backgrounds, and concerns in ways that support engagement, achievement, and empowerment." By intentionally using these guidelines as a standard for implementation across grades and subject areas, educators can be prepared to prioritize students' learning needs and begin to address some of the obstacles that schools today are encountering.

Additionally, states that are taking the initiative to prioritize the needs of diverse learners by infusing culturally responsive instruction and assessment are part of a critically important national movement to address challenges faced by our public education system. Integrating these competencies into teaching standards and practices across the country demonstrates a commitment to supporting students in their individual experiences, backgrounds, and knowledge. Moreover, this commitment communicates to all stakeholders that equitable education is a nationwide expectation for all learners and that this objective is necessary and attainable.

Appendix A

Writing Development Resources

SIX TRAITS OF EFFECTIVE WRITING ANALYSIS—MENTOR TEXT ACTIVITY

The following procedure is adapted from Gehsmann and Templeton (2022, p. 142–143).

A. **Share with your student a letter of introduction that will serve as a mentor text:**

> Hello! Our names are Samuel, Alleana, and Andrea. We are studying to become teachers. Thank you for reading and writing with us today.
>
> Samuel likes reading, kayaking, and talking to his friends. His favorite foods are sushi, chips and salsa, and quesadillas. He can cook delicious quesadillas! His favorite place is New York City. His best memory is picking up his wonderful dog Chloe from the Humane Society.
>
> Alleana likes [fill in paragraph information here].
>
> Andrea likes [fill in paragraph information here].
>
> Would you write a letter telling us about yourself and what you like?
>
> Thank you!
>
> Samuel, Alleana, and Andrea

B. **Ask the student to use your letter of introduction as a mentor text to write their own letter of introduction to you.**

COMMENTARY—SIX TRAITS ANALYSIS

Answer the questions below, providing claims about the patterns of writing you observe in student's response(s). Support your claims with examples and specific evidence related to each of the six traits of effective writing (McAndrews, 2008) (see figure A.1).

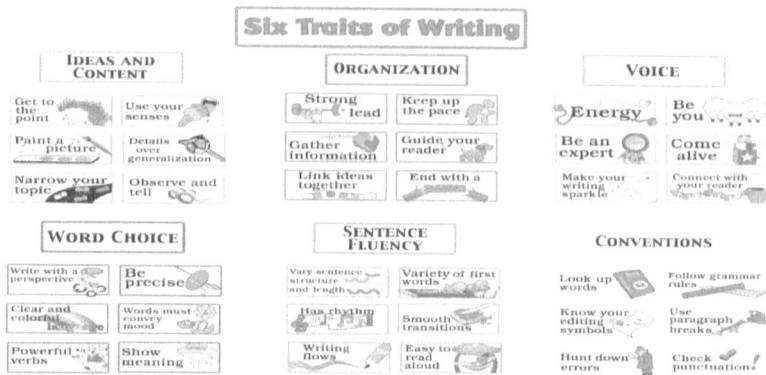

Figure A.1 Six Traits Analysis

1. What evidence of each of the six traits of writing is evident in this writer's sample?

COMMENTARY—DEVELOPMENTAL WRITING STAGE ANALYSIS

1. Referring to the stages described below, what developmental writing stage is this student writing in?
2. What kinds of reading experiences will help improve this writer's abilities?
3. What kinds of writing experiences will help improve this writer's abilities?

Writing stages encompass the development of meaning across an entire written message rather than the spelling of individual words (McAndrews, 2008).

Stage 1: Awareness, Exploration, or Role Play Writing (Drawing and scribbling)
Stage 2: Emergent (Experimenting with print conventions)
Stage 3: Transitional (Beginning to use print conventions but lacking consistency)
Stage 4: Conventional Writing (Print conventions are demonstrated with increased consistency)
Stage 5: Proficient Writing (Consistent use of print conventions/ grade-level writing) (McAndrews, 2008)
Attach digital photos of student writing sample(s).

WRITERS' WORKSHOP MODEL

Writing involves complex interactions between physical and cognitive factors. For example, writing involves the small-muscle development and eye-hand coordination needed to form letters, words, and paragraphs with a pen, pencil, or on a keyboard. Writing involves the hand, eye, and both sides of the brain for learners to make connections and construct meaning. Writing also requires familiarity with the conventions of grammar, spelling, punctuation, and form, and it necessitates a vocabulary sufficient for effective self-expression (Morrow & Gambrell, 2011).

Writing can be an entirely personal process or a social process for and with others, and it can be a way to explore thinking and create new knowledge. Regardless of intent, however, students learn to write when they are surrounded by authentic models of the writing process, have expectations that are realistic and achievable, and are allowed to make mistakes for which they receive meaningful feedback upon which they can improve. These objectives can be achieved through the writers' workshop model (Gehsmann & Templeton, 2022).

Instruction based on the writers' workshop model should follow recursive steps that can be adapted based on individual students' needs:

- Planning/Idea Building/Brainstorming
- Teacher-Led Mini Lesson (Skill isolation for formal assessment)
- Drafting
- Revising

- Editing
- Group Sharing and Publishing (Morrow & Gambrell, 2011)

Instruction based on the writers' workshop model supports written language development that follows the natural pattern of oral language development in the following ways:

- It allows for interaction between the writing process and reading experiences (e.g., letter-sound knowledge, integration of prior knowledge).
- It encourages the creation of a structure and physical environment that is conducive to writing development. For example, learners become "authors" by establishing a writing routine and through attire (hats, glasses, scarves, clipboards, feather pens) and classroom décor (candles, lamps, etc.).
- It allows learner choice and nurtures the development of the writer's voice and personal narrative. See https://www.readingrockets.org/contentfinder?search=writers%20workshop.
- It encourages the exploration of authors and genres. Topics might include visits from writers in the community (e.g., local journalists) and online author talks such as https://www.pbs.org/video/jason-reynolds-discusses-ghost-dbm4ux/.
- It is implemented in at least three class sessions per week, providing learners with the consistent writing practice that is necessary to develop writing stamina (Goodman, 1986; Gehsmann & Templeton, 2022).
- It encourages authentic assessment through mini lessons which isolate skills for formal assessment while protecting the remaining writing process for authentic assessment methods (e.g., portfolios). In this way, writers' workshops are a safe place to explore, take risks, and make changes that support natural written language development.
- It can integrate peer assessment and self-assessment through teacher-provided checklists and rubrics (Morrow & Gambrell, 2011; Peregoy & Boyle, 2017).

Appendix B

Multicultural Library Development Resources

CLASSROOM DISCUSSIONS ON RACIAL JUSTICE

https://kids.scholastic.com/content/dam/scholastic/kids/pdf/all-because-you-matter/Educator%20Guide.pdf

MULTIGRADE-LEVEL TITLE AND AUTHOR LIST

As Brave As You by Jason Reynolds
BIG by Vashti Harrison
Hair Love by Matthew Cherry and Vashti Harrison
We Are Here by Tami Charles and Bryan Collier
Gibberish by Young Vo
Mango Moon by Diane de Anda and Sye Cornelison
Max and the Talent Show by Kyle Lukoff and Luciano Lozano
Alma and How She Got Her Name by Juana Martinez-Neal
Bonnie's New Old Outfit by Madison Moore and Danielle Bennett
The Strongest Thing by Hallee Adelman and Rea Zhai
The Day Abuelo Got Lost by Diane de Anda and Alleanna Harris
The Sound of All Things by Myron Uhlberg and Ten Papoulas
All Because You Matter by Tami Charles and Bryan Collier
The People Shall Continue by Simon Ortiz and Sharol Graves
I Am Famous by Tara Luebbe, Becky Cattie, and Joanne Lew-Vriethoff

All the Way to the Top by Annette Bay Pimentel and Nabi H. Ali
Chicken Soup, Chicken Soup by Pamela Mayer and Deborah Melmon
Amy Wu and the Perfect Bao by Kat Zhang and Charlene Chua
Santiago's Dinosaurios by Mariana Rios Ramirez and Udayana Lugo
We Are Grateful by Traci Sorell and Frane Lessac
Joanna Ho by Dung Ho
Mama's Days by Andi Diehn and Angeles Ruiz
Saturday at the Food Pantry by Diane O'Neill and Brizida Magro
The Invisible Boy by Trudy Ludwig and Patrice Barton
Malik's Number Thoughts by Natalie Rompella and Alessia Girasole
Halal Hot Dogs by Susannah Aziz and Parwinder Singh
Miguel's Community Garden by JaNay Brown-Wood and Samara Hardy
Grandpa Grumps by Katrina Moore and Xindi Yan
The Coquies Still Sing by Karina Nicole Gonzalez and Krystal Quiles
We Who Produce Pearls by Joanna Ho and Amanda Phingbodhipakkiya
Bessie the Motorcycle Queen by Charles R. Smith Jr. and Charlet Kristensen
Brown Is Beautiful by Supriya Kelkar and Noor Sofi
When We Had to Leave Home by Linda Ravin Lodding and Anna Aronson
A New Year's Reunion by Yu Li-Qiong and Zhu Cheng-Liang

MULTICULTURAL CLASSROOM LIBRARY INVENTORY—EDUCATOR QUESTIONNAIRE

https://www.leeandlow.com/educators/grade-level-resources/class-room-library-questionnaire

MULTICULTURAL CLASSROOM LIBRARY INVENTORY—STUDENT QUESTIONNAIRE

Do you see people who look like you in the books in our library?	YES	NO
Are there stories in our library that are similar to stories in your life?	YES	NO
Do you see characters in the books in our library who are different from you?	YES	NO
Are there stories in our library that you are interested in reading?	YES	NO

Appendix B

Are there any stories or authors you would like to see included in our library?

1. _____
2. _____
3. _____
4. _____
5. _____

Do you have any other ideas for how we can make our library better?
_____
_____
_____
_____
_____

Appendix C

Educational History Surveys

PARENT/CAREGIVER EDUCATIONAL HISTORY SURVEY

Dear Parents and Caregivers,

Hello. I would like to welcome your family to a new school year. I feel privileged to have _____ in my class this year. I would like to know everything you are willing to share about _____ educational experiences so far. This information will help me to understand _____ unique needs, personal interests, strengths, and areas for growth. Please respond to the following questions and add any topics that will help me to create a safe and successful learning environment for _____.

Sincerely,

_____

Broadly speaking, how would you describe your child's educational experiences up to this point?

Please provide as much detail as you are comfortable with, describing how well your child's needs have been met in the following areas:

Academic—

Social—

Emotional—

Please rank your child's preference for the following subject areas (1—favorite to 7—least favorite).

_____ Language Arts and Reading

_____ Math

_____ Science

_____ Social Studies

_____ Art

_____ Physical Education

_____ Other: _____

Can you share any past experiences or specific talents/abilities that influence your child's preferences for some subjects over others?

How would you describe your child's personal literacy habits?
Does your child enjoy reading?
Does your child have a favorite genre (fiction/nonfiction/fantasy)?
What are your child's primary purposes for reading (e.g., pleasure, information seeking, or school-related)?
In what ways does your family engage in literacy activities in your community (e.g., spiritual, political, or volunteer activities)?
What kind of literacy does your child prefer (e.g., text, digital media, or visual arts)?

Does your child have any personal interests that can help me tailor my instruction to their specific preferences and motivations?

What are some areas in which I can offer your child specialized support (organizational aids, assignment reminders, extra time on assessments, group work preferences, etc.)?

Is there anything else you would like me to know about your child's educational experiences, personal preferences, and academic, social, or emotional needs?

What is the best way for me to contact you?

What is the best time of day or evening, for me to contact you?

EPP EDUCATIONAL HISTORY SURVEY

Hello and welcome to a new semester. As your professor, I would be privileged to know everything you are willing to share about your educational history. This information will help me to understand your unique needs, personal interests, strengths, and areas for growth. Please respond to the following prompts and add any topics that you feel are important.

Broadly speaking, how would you describe your K–12 educational experiences? For example, in what ways was it a positive or negative experience?

In hindsight, how well were your needs met in the following areas?

Academic—

Social—

Emotional—

What experiences, interests, and other influences have led you to pursue a profession in the field of education?

Of the subjects you will be responsible for as a K–12 educator, can you rate them from favorite to least favorite (language arts, math, science, social studies, and others)?

Do you have past experiences that have influenced your preference for some subjects over others?

How would you describe your personal literacy habits?
Do you enjoy reading?
Do you have a favorite genre?
What are your primary purposes for reading (e.g., pleasure, information seeking, or school-related)?
Do you engage in literacy activities in your community (e.g., spiritual, political, or volunteer activities)?
What kind of literacy do you prefer: textual, digital, or visual?

What are some of your personal interests that can help me tailor my instruction to your preferences and motivations?

What are some areas in which I can offer specialized support (assignment reminders, time on assessments, group work preferences, etc.)?

Is there anything else you would like me to know about your educational experiences, preferences, and needs as we begin this new semester?

References

Afflerbach, P. (2022). *Teaching readers (not reading): Moving beyond skills and strategies to reader-focused instruction*. The Guilford Press.

Aguirre, J., Mayfield-Ingram, K., & Martin, D. B. (2013). *The impact of identity in K-8 mathematics learning and teaching: Rethinking equity-based practices*. National Council of Teachers of Mathematics, Incorporated.

Alexander, P. A., & Fox, E. (2019). Reading research and practice over the decades: A historical analysis. In D. Alvermann, N. Unrau, M. Sailors, & R. B. Ruddell (Eds.), *Theoretical models and processes of literacy* (7th ed., pp. 35–64). Routledge.

August, D. (2018). Educating English learners: A review of the research. *American Educator, 42*(3), 4–39.

Auckerman, M., & Schuldt, L. C. (2021). What matters most? Toward a robust and socially just science of reading. *Reading Research Quarterly, 56*(S1), S85–S103. https://doi.org/10.1022/rrq.406.

Avineri, N., Johnson, E., Brice-Heath, S., McCarty, T., Ochs, E., Kremer-Sadlik, T., & Paris, D. (2015). Invited forum: Bridging the "language gap". *Journal of Linguistic Anthropology, 25*(1), 66–86.

Bacon, H. R., & Kaya, J. (2018). Imagined communities and identities: A spaciotemporal discourse analysis of one woman's literacy journey. *Linguistics and Education, 46*, 82–90.

Banks, J. A. (2016). *Cultural diversity and education: Foundations, curriculum, and teaching*. Routledge.

Banks, J. (2020). *Diversity, transformative knowledge, and civic education*. Routledge.

Beck, I. L., McKeown, M. G., & Kucan, L. (2013). *Bringing words to life: Robust vocabulary instruction* (2nd ed.). Guilford.

Benavot, A. (2015). Literacy in the 21st century: Towards a dynamic nexus of social relations. *International Review of Education, 61*, 273–294.

Berliner, D. (2013a). Sorting out the effects of inequality and poverty, teachers and schooling on America's youth. In S. L. Nichols (Ed.), *Educational policy and the socialization of youth for the 21st century* (pp. 1–26). Teachers College Press.

Berliner, D. C. (2013b). Effects of inequality and poverty vs. teachers and schooling on America's youth. *Teachers College Record, 116*(1). Retrieved from https://www.tcrecord.org/Content.asp?ContentId=16889.

Boaler, J. (2008). Promoting 'relational equity' and high mathematics achievement through an innovative mixed-ability approach. *British Educational Research Journal, 34*(2), 167–194.

Bondie, R. S., Dahnke, C., & Zusho, A. (2019). How does changing "one-size-fits-all" to differentiated instruction affect teaching? *Review of Research in Education, 43*(1), 336–362.

Brion, C. (2021). Creating intentionally inviting school cultures during crisis. *Journal of Interdisciplinary Studies in Education, 10*(1), 160–181.

Brown, K. D., & Brown, A. L. (2012). Useful and dangerous discourses: Deconstructing racialized knowledge about African-American students. *Educational Foundations, Winter-Spring, 26*, 11–26.

Brown, K. D. (2014). Teaching in color: A critical race theory in education analysis of the literature on preservice teachers of color and teacher education in the US. *Race Ethnicity and Education, 17*(3), 326–345.

Caraballo, L. (2014). The student as assemblage of success: Constructing multiple identities amidst classed, gendered, and raced discourses of achievement. *Curriculum and Teaching Dialogue, 16*(1/2), 103.

Carnevale, A. P., Fasules, M. L., Quinn, M. C., & Campbell, K. P. (2019). Born to win, schooled to lose: Why equally talented students don't get equal chances to be all they can be. *Georgetown University Center on Education and the Workforce*, Executive Summary, pp. 1–22.

Castles, A., Rastle, K., & Nation, K. (2018). Ending the reading wars: Reading Acquisition from novice to expert. *Association for Psychological Science, 19*(1), 5–51.

Cole, M. W. (2019). Translanguaging in every classroom. *Language Arts, 96*(4), 244–249.

Collier, V. P., & Thomas, W. P. (2017). Validating the power of bilingual schooling: Thirty-two years of large-scale, longitudinal research. *Annual Review of Applied Linguistics, 37*, 203–217. https://www.cambridge.org/core/journals/annual-review-of-applied-linguistics/article/abs/validating-the

-power-of-bilingual-schooling-thirtytwo-years-of-largescale-longitudinal-research/909F284BFF9C327124AD08987143E677.

Compton-Lilly, C., Spence, L. K., Thomas, P. L., & Decker, S. L. (2023). Stories grounded in decades of research: What we truly know about the teaching of reading. *International Literacy Association*, 1–10. https://doi.org/10.1002/trtr.2258.

Dack, H., & Tomlinson, C. A. (2015). Inviting all student to learn. *Educational Leadership, 72*(6), 10–15.

Degen, R. J. (2014). Brain-based learning: The neurological findings about the human brain that every teacher should know to be effective. *Amity Global Business Review*, 9, 15–23. Retrieved from http://www.amity.edu/aibs/Researchpublication.asp.

Derman-Sparks, L., Edwards, J. O., & Goins, C. M. (2020). *Anti-bias education for young children & ourselves*. NAEYC.

Dewey, J. (1938). *Experience and education*. Macmillan.

Duke, N. K., & Cartwright, K. B. (2021). The science of reading progresses: Communicating advances beyond the simple view of reading. *Reading Research Quarterly, 56*, S25–S44.

Elleman, A. M., & Oslund E. L. (2019). Reading comprehension research: Implications for practice and policy. *Policy Insights from the Behavioral and Brain Sciences, 6*(1), 3–11. https://doi.org/10.1177/2372732218816339.

Elliot, A. J. (1999). Approach and avoidance motivation and achievement goals. *Educational Psychologist, 34*(3), 169–189.

Elliot, A. J., & Dweck, C. S. (2005). *Handbook of competence and motivation*. Guildford Press.

Endres, T., Carpenter, S., Martin, A., & Renkl, A. (2017). Enhancing learning by retrieval: Enriching free recall with elaborative prompting. *Learning and Instruction, 49*, 13–20.

ESSA. (2015a). Every Student Succeeds Act of 2015, Pub. L. No. 114-95 § 114 Stat. 1177 (2015–2016).

ESSA. (2015b). Actions – S. 1177 – 114th Congress (2015–2016). https://www.congress.gov/bill/114th-congress/senate-bill/1177/all-actions.

ESSA Federal Funding Guide. (2018). Retrieved from http://myschoolmyvoice.nea.org/essa-federal-funding-guide/.

Faltis, C. J., & Valdes, G. (2016). Preparing teachers for teaching in and advocating for linguistically diverse classrooms: A vade mecum for teacher educators. In *Handbook of research on teaching* (pp. 549–592). http://dx.doi.org/10.3102/978-0-935302-48-6.

Freire, P. (1990). *Pedagogy of the oppressed*. Continuum.

Gabriel, R. (2018). The straw man in the new round of the reading wars. *The Washington Post, August*, 1–7.

Garcia, E., & Weiss, E. (2015). Early education gaps by social class and race start U.S. children out on unequal footing. *Economic Policy Institute*, Report, 1–10.

Garcia, O., Johnson, S. L., & Seltzer, K. (2017). *The translanguaging classroom: Leveraging student bilingualism for learning*. Caslon.

Gay, G. (2013). Teaching to and through cultural diversity. *Curriculum Inquiry, 43*(1), 48–70.

Gay, G. (2018). *Culturally responsive teaching: Theory, research and practice* (3rd ed.). Teachers College Press.

Gee, J. P. (2008). *Social Linguistics and literacies: Ideologies and discourses*. Routledge.

Gee, J. P. (2014). *An introduction to discourse analysis: Theory and method*. Routledge.

Gehsmann, K. M., & Templeton, S. (2022). *Teaching reading and writing: The developmental approach*. Pearson.

González, N. (2016). Imagining literacy equity: Theorizing flows of community practices. *Literacy research: theory, method, and practice, 65*(1), 69–93.

Goodman, Y. M. (1986). Children coming to know literacy. In W. H. Teale & E. Sulzby (Eds.), *Emergent literacy: Writing and reading* (pp. 1–14). Ablex.

Goodman, Y. M. (2014). Nu!...so!...where do we go from here? In K. S. Goodman, R. C. Calfee, & Y. M. Goodman (Eds.), *Whose knowledge counts in government literacy policies?* (pp. 201–206). Routledge.

Guthrie, J. T., Taboada, A., & Wigfield, A. (2010). Alignment of cognitive processes in reading with motivations for reading (Chapter 18). In Fisher, D., & Lapp, D. (Eds.), *Handbook of Research on Teaching the English Language Arts: Sponsored by the International Reading Association and the National Council of Teachers of English* (3rd ed., pp. 125–131). Routledge. https://doi.org/10.4324/9780203839713.

Gutierrez, K. D. & Rogoff, B. (2003). Cultural ways of learning: Individual traits of repertoires of practices. *Educational Researcher, 32*(5), 19–25.

Halliday, M. A. K. (1994). The place of dialogue in children's construction of meaning. In R. Ruddell, M. Ruddell, & H. Singer (Eds.), *Theoretical models and processes of reading* (4th ed., pp. 133–145). International Reading Association.

Hambacher, E., Silva, B., & Morelli, G. (2020). "There was complete silence": Reflections on teacher preparation for social justice education in a predominantly white community. *Multicultural Perspectives, 22*(4), 201–209.

Hammond, Z. (2015). *Culturally responsive teaching and the brain: Promoting authentic engagement and rigor among culturally and linguistically diverse students*. Corwin Press.

Haas, E., Huang, M., Tran L., & Yu, A. (2016). *The achievement progress of EL students in Nevada* (REL 2016-154). Regional Educational Laboratory Program. http://ies.ed.gov/ncee/edlabs.

Heath, S. B. (1982). What no bedtime story means: Narrative skills at home and school. *Language in society, 11*(1), 49–76.

Heath, S. B. (1983). *Ways with words: Language, life, and work in communities and classrooms.* Cambridge University Press.

Howlett, K. M., Bowles, F. A., & Lincoln, F. (2017). Infusing multicultural literature into teacher education programs: Three instructional approaches. *Multicultural Education, 24*, 10–15.

Hruby, G. G., & Goswami, U. (2011). Neuroscience and reading: A review for reading education researchers. *Reading Research Quarterly, 46*(2), 156–172.

Illinois State Board of Education. (n.d.). *Culturally responsive teaching and learning standards.* https://www.isbe.net/Pages/Culturally-Responsive-Teaching-Leading-Standards.aspx.

Jackson, V. T. (2016). *Promoting student achievement through educational practices in middle school math transitioning classrooms.* Northcentral University.

Jensen, E. (2008). *Brain-based learning: The new paradigm of teaching* (2nd ed.). Corwin Press.

Kalmakis, K. A., & Chandler, G. E. (2015). Health consequences of adverse childhood experiences: A systematic review. *Journal of the American Association of Nurse Practitioners, 27*(8), 457–465.

Kane, B., & Savitz, R.S. (2022). Disciplinary literacy and culturally sustaining pedagogies: Tensions and potential. In S. Chambers Cantrell, D. Walker-Dalhouse, & A. Lazar (Eds.), *Culturally sustaining literacy pedagogies: Honoring students' heritages, literacies, and languages* (pp. 53–74). Teachers College Press.

Kelly, L. B., Wakefield, W., Caires-Hurley, J., Kganetso, L. W., Moses, L., & Baca, E. (2021). What is culturally informed literacy instruction? A review of research in p–5 contexts. *Journal of Literacy Research, 53*(1), 75–99. https://doi.org/10.1177/1086296X20986602.

Kendi, I. X. (2023). *How to be an antiracist.* Penguin Random House.

Kganesto, L. M. W. (2016). Creating and using culturally sustaining informational texts. *The Reading Teacher, 70*(4), 445–455.

Kim, S., & Morita-Mullaney, T. (2020). When preparation matters: A mixed method study of in-service teacher preparation to serve English learners. *Mid-Western Educational Researcher, 32*(3), 231–254. https://scholarworks.bgsu.edu/mwer/vol32/iss3/4.

Kohn, A. (2015). What 'No Child Left Behind' left behind. [Blog post]. http://www.alfiekohn.org/blogs/nclb/.

Kolano, L. Q., Davila, L. T., LaChance, J., & Coffey, H. (2014). Multicultural teacher education: Why teachers say it matters in preparing them for English language learners. *The CATESOL Journal, 25*(1), 41–65.

Kramsch, C. (2009). Cultural perspectives on language learning and teaching. *Handbook of foreign language communication and learning, 6*, 219–245.

Krashen, S. (1982). *Principles and practices in second language acquisition.* Pergamon Press.

Ladson-Billings, G. (2021a). Three decades of culturally relevant, responsive, & sustaining pedagogy: What lies ahead? *The Educational Forum, 85*(4), 351–354.

Ladson-Billings, G. (2021b). *Culturally relevant pedagogy: Asking a different question.* Teachers College Press.

Lantolf, J. P., & Thorne, S. L. (2006). *Sociocultural theory and the genesis of second language development.* Oxford University Press.

Leider, C. M., Colombo, M. W., & Nerlino, E. (2021). Decentralization, teacher quality, and the education of English learners: Do State education agencies effectively prepare teachers of ELs? *Education Policy Analysis Archives, 29*(100), 1–44. https://doi.org/10.14507/epaa.29.5279.

Lopez, F., & Santibanez, L. (2018). Teacher preparation for emergent bilingual students: Implications of evidence for policy. *Education Policy Analysis Archives, 26*(36), 1–41. https://doi.org/10.14507/epaa.26.2866.

Loveless, T. (2018). *Why standards produce weak reform.* American Enterprise Institute. http://www.aei.org/events/bush-obama-school-reform-lessons-learned/.

Ludvik, M. J. B. (Ed.). (2023). *The neuroscience of learning and development: Enhancing creativity, compassion, critical thinking, and peace in higher education.* Taylor & Francis.

Maguire-Jack, K., Font, S., Dillard, R., & Dvalishvilli, S. B. (2021). Neighborhood poverty and wadverse childhood experiences over the first 15 years of life. *International Journal of Child Maltreatment, 4*, 93–114. https://doi.org/10.1007/s42448-021-00072-y.

Martin, D. B., Gholson, M. L., & Leonard, J. (2010). Mathematics as gatekeeper: Power and privilege in the production of knowledge. *Journal of Urban Mathematics Education, 3*(2), 12–24.

McAndrews, S. L. (2008). *Diagnostic literacy assessments and instructional strategies: A literacy specialist's resource.* International Reading Association.

Medina, J. (2008). *Brain rules: 12 principles for surviving and thriving at work, home, and school.* Pear Press.

Milner, H. R. (2021). *Start where you are, but don't stay there: Understanding diversity, opportunity gaps, and teaching in today's classrooms.* Harvard Education Press.

Moll, L. C., Amanti, C., Neff, D., & Gonzalez, N. (1992). Funds of knowledge for teaching: Using a qualitative approach to connect homes and classrooms. *Theory into Practice, 31*(2), 132–141.

Morita-Mullaney, T. (2019). At the intersection of bilingual specialty and leadership: A collective case study of district leadership for emergent bilinguals. *Bilingual Research Journal, 40*(1), 31–53. https://doi.org/10.1080/15235882.2018.1563005.

Morrow, L. M., & Gambrell, L. B. (2011). *Best practices in literacy instruction.* The Guilford Press.

Moss, P. A., Pullin, D., Gee, J. P., & Haertel, E. H. (2005). The idea of testing: Psychometric and sociocultural perspectives. *Measurement, 3*(2), 63–83.

Muhammad, G. (2023). *Unearthing joy: A guide to culturally and historically responsive teaching and learning.* Scholastic.

Muñiz, J. (2019). *Culturally responsive teaching: A 50-state survey of teaching standards.* New America.

Najarro, I. (2023, February 21). The English learner population is growing: Is teacher training keeping pace? *Education Week.* https://www.edweek.org/teaching-learning/the-english-learner-population-is-growing-is-teacher-training-keeping-pace/2023/02#:~:text=And%20teachers%20generally%20seem%20to,and%2061%20percent%20said%20no.

National Center for Education Statistics, U.S. Department of Education. (2020). *English language learners in public schools.* https://nces.ed.gov/programs/coe/indicator_cgf.asp.

National Center for Education Statistics, U.S. Department of Education. (2024). *English learners in public schools.* https://nces.ed.gov/programs/coe/indicator/cgf/english-learners.

National Reading Panel (U.S.), & National Institute of Child Health and Human Development (U.S.). (2000). *Report of the National Reading Panel: Teaching children to read: An evidence-based assessment of the scientific research literature on reading and its implications for reading instruction: Reports of the subgroups.* National Institute of Child Health and Human Development, National Institutes of Health.

Nieto, Sonia. (1992). *Affirming diversity: The sociopolitical context of multicultural education.* Longman Publishing Company.

Office of Civil Rights. (1970). Memo regarding language minority children. https://nces.ed.gov/programs/coe/pdf/Indicator-CGF/coe_cgf_2013_05.pdf.

Ogbu, J. U. (1995). Cultural problems in minority education: Their interpretations and consequences—Part one: Theoretical background. *The Urban Review, 27*(3), 189–205.

Pacheco, M., & Gutierrez, K. (2009). Cultural-historical approaches to literacy teaching and learning. In C. Compton-Lilly (Ed.), *Breaking the silence:*

Recognizing the social and cultural resources students bring to classrooms (pp. 60–77). International Reading Association.
Parks, A. N. (2009). Rethinking the deployment of the 'achievement gap' in equity arguments. *For the Learning of Mathematics, 29*(1), 14-19.
Paulick, J., Kibler, A. K., & Palacios, N. (2023). Understanding literacies in Latinx families: Teachers using home visits to reimagine classroom practices. *The Reading Teacher, 76*(5), 578–585. https://doi.org/10.1002/trtr.2178.
Peregoy, S., & Boyle, O. (2017). *Reading, writing, and learning in ESL: A resource book for teaching k– 12 English learners* (7th ed.). Pearson Education, Inc.
Perry, K. (2012). What is literacy? A critical overview of sociocultural perspectives. *Journal of Language and Literacy Education, 8*(1), 50–71.
Polat, N. H. (2011). A comparative analysis of pre-and in-service teacher beliefs about readiness and self-competency: Revisiting teacher education for ELLs. *System, 38*(2), 228–244. https://doi.org/10.1016/j.system.2010.03.004.
Ramirez, G., Chang, H., Maloney, E. A., Levine, S. C., & Beilock, S. L. (2016). On the relationship between math anxiety and math achievement in early elementary school: The role of problem-solving strategies. *Journal of experimental child psychology, 141*, 83–100.
Reeves, D. (2016). *Elements of grading: A guide to effective practice* (2nd ed.). Solution Tree Press.
Reinking, D., Hruby, G. G., & Risko, V. J. (2023). Legislating phonics: Settled science or political polemics? *Teachers College Record, 125*(1), 104–131. https://doi.org/10.1177/01614681231155688.
Rothstein, R. (2011). Grading the education reformers. *Economic Policy Institute, August*, 1–5.
Routman, R. (2000). *Conversations: Strategies for teaching, learning, and evaluating*. Heinemann Publishing.
Routman, R. (2018). *Literacy essentials: Engagement, excellence, and equity for all learners*. Stenhouse Publishers.
Sanchez-Ruiz, M. J., Perez-Gonzalez, J. C., Romo, M., & Matthews, G. (2015). Divergent thinking and stress dimensions. *Thinking Skills and Creativity, 17*, 102–116.
Santora, L. E., Baker, S. K., Fien, H., Smith, J. L. M., & Chard, D. J. (2016). Using read-alouds to help struggling readers access and comprehend complex, informational text. *Teaching Exceptional Children, 48*(6), 282–292.
Scarborough, H. S. (2001). Connecting early language and literacy to later reading (dis)abilities: Evidence, theory, and practice. In S. Neuman & D. Dickinson (Eds.), *Handbook for research in early literacy* (pp. 97–110). Guilford Press.

Shanahan, T. (2020). What constitutes a science of reading instruction? *Reading Research Quarterly, 55*(S1), S235–S247. https://doi.org/10.1002/rrq.349.

Shannon, P. (2014). Re-reading poverty: Reorienting educational policy. In Goodman, K. S., Calfee, R. C., & Goodman, Y. M. (Eds.), *Whose knowledge counts in government literacy policies?* (pp. 3–46). Routledge.

Shepard, L. A. (2016). Testing and assessment for the good of education: Contributions of AERA presidents, 1915–2015. *Educational Researcher, 45*(2), 112–121.

Sibold, C. (2011). Building English language learners' academic vocabulary: Strategies & tips. *Multicultural Education*, Winter, 24–28.

Sleeter, C. E. (2012). Confronting the marginalization of culturally responsive pedagogy. *Urban Education, 47*(3), 562–584.

Smagorinsky, P. (2001). If meaning is constructed, what is it made from? Toward a cultural theory of reading. *Review of Educational Research, 71*(1), 133–169.

Smagorinsky, P. (2013). What does Vygotsky provide for the 21st century language arts teacher? *Language Arts, 90*(3), 192–204.

Sousa, D. A., & Tomlinson, C. A. (2018). Differentiation and the brain: How Neuroscience supports the learner-friendly classroom (2nd ed.). Solution Tree Press.

Spielhagen, F. R. (2015). *The algebra solution to mathematics reform: Completing the equation.* Teachers College Press.

Steele, H., Bates, J., Steele, M., Dube, S. R., Danskin, K., Knafo, H., Nikitiades, K. B., Meissner, P., & Murphy, A. (2016). Adverse childhood experiences, poverty, and parenting stress. *Canadian Journal of Behavioural Science*, 1–29. https://dx.doi.org/10.1037/cbs0000034.

Street, B. (2013). Literacy in theory and practice: Challenges and debates over 50 years. *Theory Into Practice, 52*, 52–62.

Title IV of the Civil Rights Act of 1964: Desegregation of Public Education (1964).

Tomlinson, C. A. (2017). *How to differentiate instruction in academically diverse classrooms* (3rd ed.). Association for Supervision and Curriculum Development.

Torff, B. (2014). Folk belief theory, the rigor gap, and the achievement gap. *The Educational Forum, 78*, 174–189. https://doi.org/10.1080/00131725.2013.878424.

Torff, B., & Murphy, A. F. (2020). Teachers' beliefs about English learners: Adding linguistic support to enhance academic rigor. *Phi Delta Kappan, 101*(5), 14–18.

Torgerson, C., Brooks, G., Gascoine, L., & Higgins, S. (2019). Phonics: Reading policy and the evidence of effectiveness from a systematic `tertiary' review. *Research Papers in Education, 34* (2), 208–238. https://doi.org/10.1080/02671522.2017.1420816.

United States Census Bureau. (2023, November 9). *U.S. population projected to begin declining in second half of century* [Press release]. https://www.census.gov/newsroom/press-releases/2023/population-projections.html.

Van Der Veer, R. (2007). Vygotsky in context: 1900–1935. In Daniels, H., Cole, M., & Wertsch, J. V. (Eds.), *The Cambridge companion to Vygotsky* (pp. 21–49). Cambridge University Press.

Walker, V. S. (2020). *The lost education of Horace Tate: Uncovering the hidden heroes who fought for justice in schools.* The New Press.

Wei, Y., Hovey, K. A., Gerzel-Short, L., Hsiao, Y. J., Miller, R. D., & Kelly, J. H. (2022). Culturally responsive and high-leverage practices: Facilitating effective instruction for English learners with learning disabilities. *TESOL Journal, 14*(e697), 1–15. https://doi.org/10.1002/tesj.697.

Witt, P. G. (2016). Teaching first graders to comprehend complex texts through read-alouds. *The Reading Teacher, 70*(1), 29–38.

Woulfin, S. L., & Gabriel, R. (2022). Big waves on the rocky shore: A discussion of reading policy, infrastructure, and implementation in the era of the science of reading. *The Reading Teacher, 76*(3), 326–332. https://doi.org/10.1002/trtr.2153.

Wilburn, G., Cramer, B., & Walton, E. (n.d.). The great divergence: Growing disparities between the nation's highest and lowest achievers in NAEP mathematics and reading between 2009 and 2019. *NAEPPLUS+*.[Blog post]. https://nces.ed.gov/nationsreportcard/blog/mathematics_reading_2019.aspx.

World Literacy Foundation. (2015). *The economic and social cost of illiteracy: A snapshot of illiteracy in a global context.* https//worldliteracyfoundation.org/wp-content/uploads/2015/02/WLF-FINAL-ECONOMIC-REPORT.pdf.

About the Authors

Susan Foster, PhD, is an assistant professor of elementary education in the School of Education, Health, and Human Behavior at Southern Illinois University Edwardsville. Dr. Foster teaches courses in literacy, differentiated instruction, and second language acquisition and learning. Before coming to SIUE, Dr. Foster supervised the *America Reads Challenge* literacy program at Southern Illinois University Carbondale and taught elementary and middle school in Springfield, Illinois.

Dr. Barbara Martin is an associate professor of teaching and learning in the School of Education, Health, and Human Behavior at Southern Illinois University Edwardsville. Dr. Martin teaches courses in teacher preparation and conducts research in technology integration, math methods, and STEM-related fields.

www.ingramcontent.com/pod-product-compliance
Lightning Source LLC
Chambersburg PA
CBHW021813220426
43662CB00006B/299